Data Structure Synthesis

USING MATHEMATICS IN DATABASE DESIGN TO ENRICH APPLICATION PERFORMANCE, BUSINESS ANALYSIS, AND DATA SCIENCE

Doug Needham

Technics Publications
SEDONA, ARIZONA

115 Linda Vista, Sedona, AZ 86336 USA
https://www.TechnicsPub.com

Edited by Sadie Hoberman

Cover design by Lorena Molinari

First Printing 2024

ISBN, print ed.   9781634625746
ISBN, Kindle ed.   9781634625753
ISBN, PDF ed.   9781634625760

Library of Congress Control Number: 2024946218

To my daughter, Kori Leigh Needham, my eternal research assistant, sounding board, and sidekick.
Thank you for always being there for me.

To my dad, Douglas Vernon Needham. Even though we do not speak enough, as I began to tackle this manuscript, the refrain of "This is my story" inspired me to tell things the way I tell them in this book.

To the Angel of Florence, thank you for letting me bend your ear.

Contents

Foreword

Unlocking New Insights in Data Engineering

It's been many years since I first met Doug Needham as a student in my Data Vault 2.0 class. From the beginning, Doug stood out with his remarkable ability to think critically and ask the kinds of questions that challenge and deepen our understanding of complex data models. His curiosity wasn't just about grasping the core concepts of Data Vault—he sought to understand the deeper mathematical foundations and the nuances of methodology, implementation, and model construction.

What continues to impress me about Doug's work is his unique ability to take abstract ideas and apply mathematical rigor to them in ways that unveil hidden patterns and possibilities. I often tasked him with the challenge of finding mathematical explanations for the existence of Data Vault models. Not only did Doug rise to the occasion, but he also developed algorithms that score metadata, reveal relationships, and discover new insights about models and data—insights that might otherwise go unnoticed.

This book is the culmination of Doug's work and thoughts, and it offers something fundamental to our field. It forwards the conversation on data engineering and data science, especially in the realm of model discovery and advancement. By leveraging the power of metadata, Doug has shown how we can unlock new levels of understanding and innovation in data architecture.

I believe this book will inspire you, as it has inspired me, to see data and its relationships in a new light. I hope you find the same satisfaction in exploring Doug's work that I have had over the years of watching his growth as both a thinker and a practitioner in the field. It is a privilege to witness the contributions Doug has made, and I am confident his work will continue to drive advancements in data science and data engineering.

Happy reading!

Dan Linstedt
CEO, DataVaultAlliance Holdings LLC

Introduction

"There is math behind this technique!" Dan Linstedt exclaimed as he explained the principles of data vault modeling to the training session attendees.

I raised my hand to interrupt him.

"What is the math behind this? Can you explain it?" I asked from the back of the room.

"I do not know. I am a concepts guy, but I know this works because it has been implemented repeatedly."

I sat disappointed as I tried to grasp what he meant. Little did I know that this simple exchange would set me on a path that would, in many ways, define the rest of my career.

Inspiration comes in many forms. As I will share in detail in the section on my journey, I started my career in the Marines. During my time there, I worked on mainframe databases. I learned a lot from many mentors, including database layout, design, implementation, operations, maintenance, etc.

I learned everything necessary to manage a production database for any size enterprise. I did not know then that I had only learned one way of doing things. I continued studying, referring quite often to Codd[1] and Date[2].

---

[1] https://en.wikipedia.org/wiki/Edgar_F._Codd

[2] https://en.wikipedia.org/wiki/Christopher_J._Date

Unfortunately, I realized that in the real world, Application Divas ("app divas") do database design, who may or may not have studied the fundamentals or had proper training.

For nearly all of history, human lives have been governed primarily by ignorance. A cleric, priest, king, ruler, autocrat, or someone who seems successful in one domain claims the ultimate authority, deciding things for everyone else. These people may actually be ignorant in many subjects, but because of their position, others listen to and follow their "authority."

Lead application developers embrace this autocracy. They know how an application language works. As such, they know how to make things happen within the slim domain that an application is responsible for. In an enterprise, many domains are homegrown and off the shelf. The data stored in these repositories is more important to the organization's long-term health than any individual application.

Having experts in the data management domain balance out these high-priests serves an organization's best interest.

In my experience, app divas do not like to hear that your expertise matches or exceeds theirs, even when a poorly designed database fails catastrophically due to scaling, physical constraints, poor queries, or any other of the thousands of reasons that database administrators and now DataOps professionals work to prevent. Most application teams violate David Ricardo's law of comparative advantage by always insisting that they do every part of an application including the development of the data model.[3]

This book explores what I have learned and my experiences in understanding why things work as they do in a production database.

There is a bit of math involved. I will not promise to ignore the math, but I will promise to make it appropriate for the topic at hand. I will specifically show how synthesizing these mathematical concepts with proper design fundamentals can produce data products that meet and exceed the requirements of the modern business world.

I strongly believe that understanding how a technology evolved enhances the ability to apply it.

Is it crucial to understand that a loom was an inspiration for the concept of a programmable machine to be able to use it effectively?

NO!

Anyone can use these programmable machines without knowing this information. Isaac Newton said, "If I have seen further, it is by standing on the shoulders of giants." We stand today on the shoulders of the giants that have come before us. But, we do not just stand on their shoulders.

---

[3] https://en.wikipedia.org/wiki/Comparative_advantage

As we understand their journey, the challenges they faced, and the problems they were trying to solve, we not only learn how to solve a problem but why they needed to pick up their tools, pack a lunch, and start down the road of discovery.

This gives us not only a different perspective of our own reality, but also shows how and why these humans who were considered at one time to be normal or typical became the giants we should all admire.

Only a few will undertake the hero's journey to change THE world.
All of us can undertake the hero's journey to change OUR world.

Hopefully, we can also help others along the way and make a positive difference in other people's lives to help them take a few more steps along their journey. Helping others be themselves and find their destiny always improves our own livelihoods.

When you finish this book and have learned new ways to think about a data system, please share this with others. Please contact me to share your experiences and how this has helped you.

One

My Journey Here

"It's not that I'm so smart, it's just that I stay with problems longer." - Albert Einstein

Why should anyone listen to me?

In most technical books, the author presents himself to the audience with a brief introduction laying out their credentials: Ph.D from some institution, master's degree in technical stuff, and research on such and such topic to be discussed in the manuscript.

Spoiler alert: no sheepskin is hanging at the end of this introduction journey.

Instead, I am sharing the journey that became my most valuable credential.

This unexpected journey into the world of mathematics evolved from decisions made on my behalf by many others, some of whom wanted to protect me, some of whom did not. We can understand the discoveries I made later in life in the context of what was going on in my life, starting with my lack of formal education in the mathematical arts.

My journey was searching for not just a solution but why the solutions work.

All the math I will discuss in the rest of this book was discovered by many other people, most of whom worked together over centuries to build on each other's work.

My role in this journey involves applying what may be considered sophisticated mathematics to the mundane world of data management.

In the world of data management, a simple data structure is a table. Based on the work of Codd and Date, this table structure is itself a Predicate. This Predicate describes what the Data Structure encapsulates. Since it is a mathematical object, we can think of this predicate as a Category composed of subcomponents.

The synthesis of mathematical concepts with data structure organization can itself lead to some interesting ways of thinking about data organization.

The Predicate itself can be analyzed, decomposed, broken apart, or even combined with other Predicates to enrich the meaning of the data being represented.

For example, the performance of a query on a wide table could be better. Chances are multiple predicates are stored in a single data structure, they need to be separated into their own entities. Attempting to transform data from a set of tables into multiple predicates at the same time can lead to performance issues. In contrast, if you break apart the predicates into separate transformation processes, the system's overall performance improves.

Organizing related predicates together in patterns can yield exciting results. For example, a dimensional data model is an application of combinatorics.

Other mathematical objects, such as functions, can describe the relationships between multiple Predicates. This is well-known, but I have not seen many instances of this fundamental concept in the practice of data management. What I have seen are complicated processes trying to learn the relationship between multiple types of objects (Customers, Visitors, Orders, Products, and the like).

My claim is that a well-designed set of data structures that encapsulate and visualize an organization's data flows can be used as a blueprint for learning the details of these relationships, so long as proper design is done and the Data Structures themselves are built following the best practices outlined in this and many other books that discuss Data Management best practices.

I hope to contribute to the state-of-the-art of managing, organizing, and analyzing Data Structures. It is up to you, the reader, to judge whether I have accomplished this goal.

Early life

Every decision you make has consequences. I chose not to suffer the punishment for what I knew to be correct, and I decided not to be bullied.

I chose to fight back.

The consequences of those decisions shaped my future in ways that an elementary school student could never comprehend at the time.

This story is about a journey that involves reading many books, taking online classes, attending lectures, self-studying, and experimenting.

I am a late bloomer. My passion for mathematics formed late in life—at least, that is what I realize now. In many ways, my love for mathematics was stifled by many circumstances from a young age. It was stifled as the result of my decision not to be bullied in public school. Since I was fighting back against being bullied, my parents pulled me out of public school and put me into a religious school. Most people, when you talk about being in a religious school, think of a Catholic school. This school was not a Catholic school.

It was worse.

It was an independent Baptist school.

In the South.

In Texas.

As much as I disliked this type of schooling, there were a few things I learned how to do.

Read, read critically, and solve problems by myself. The kind of school I was in did not require the teachers to be adept at the subject they were teaching. I usually wanted to know more than what was explained in lectures. I had to do my research to understand quite a few topics better.

However, these skills would serve me well throughout my career.

When I was a child, you would not have anticipated I would end up working with mathematics and computer technology. I did art projects, macrame, weaving, sewing, and theater.

As I began learning programming and some of the history of computers, this more artistic background gave me an understanding of how the ideas formed to create our current computer age.

I was never good at drawing or painting; I just enjoyed it. One school I transferred to had a class available called mechanical drawing that I was immediately drawn to.[4] (CAD software has since replaced mechanical drawing.)

In the real world, when you create a mechanical drawing, it is on a piece of paper. This makes it two-dimensional. One of the challenges of mechanical drawing is representing three dimensions in two dimensions. Very similar to artistic drawings and paintings, things like perspective,

---

[4] https://history.nasa.gov/diagrams/shuttle.htm

viewpoint, and foreshortening are used in mechanical drawing to represent three-dimensional objects in two dimensions. It becomes essential which drawn line is "on top" of another or "in front of" another. This is usually represented by the things around the point at which the two lines meet. Shading, erasing parts of a line, or another indicator drawn onto the paper makes the point for the observer.

Since a mechanical engineer takes these drawings and builds the thing drawn, the perspective, which line represents the top, bottom, front, or back, becomes essential. After all, trying to create a physical implementation of Escher's Stairs[5] can be problematic.

While this class was fun and easy for me, the lessons I learned came back to mind many years after I thought I had forgotten them.

Life requires balance. Just as there are things you may enjoy in school, there are things you may not. In addition to this drawing class taught by someone who had worked as an actual drafter in the real world, we had an English teacher. She was a lovely lady, but her favorite topic to teach was sentence diagramming.[6] For those who need to learn a sentence diagram, the idea is to break a sentence apart into its grammatical structure: Nouns, Verbs, Subjects, Direct Objects, Objects, and on and on.

---

[5] https://en.wikipedia.org/wiki/Relativity_(M._C._Escher)

[6] https://en.wikipedia.org/wiki/Sentence_diagram

This homework became mind-numbingly boring the more we did it. You read a sentence, break it apart, and diagram it. Then you read another sentence, break it apart, diagram it, and Zzz.

I remember a few of us asking at different times how this would help us or be helpful in the real world.

Other than the general "do this because I told you to do it" answers, her most helpful answer was something like: *This will help you mentally structure what you are trying to say or write in the future.* You may not diagram a sentence again, but knowing the structure of how to organize a sentence is like muscle memory. You will eventually use this unconsciously.

I doubted her answer, but I did the homework like any student. While I did not embrace this technique, I understood it sufficiently to pass the class. I assumed I would never use this technique in the real world.

I was wrong again.

Growing up in Southeast Texas near Houston, Johnson Space Center was always appealing for grade school field trips. At some point in the late 1970s, one of the schools I attended took a day trip to tour the facility. Like any grade school trip, I have vague memories of most of the trip.

I do have specific memories of seeing the computer room. They said this is where we do all the calculations that got us to the moon.

I was starstruck.

I knew one day I would be able to work with computers like that.

After I had spent my time in the limbo of a Southern Baptist education, I returned to public school in my sophomore year. I learned that my high school had a mainframe in the vocational school.

Even in the late eighties, working on a mainframe was considered a trade vocation. I should have paid more attention to that.

Nevertheless, I walked into a large classroom on the first day of class. One room contained standard desks and a chalkboard. The room next door was the "lab," a long room divided in two. The smaller portion had TRS-80s, Apple ||'s, and other "small systems." The more significant portion of the room had my heart when I walked in.

In this room, on a raised computer room floor, sat an IBM 370-115 mainframe. It had a master console, punched card reader, card punch machine, four spinning DASD (direct access storage devices) disks, and other peripherals that supported the system. Along the walls, in thick three-ring binders, sat manual after manual that covered how to operate this enormous machine.

It had a specific start-up sequence called the IPL (initial program load) procedure. You would turn the disk devices on before the CPU. The card reader had to be started and loaded with punched cards to start processing, etc.

As each component came to life, the dull roar that hummed in the room made it seem exciting. When one of the students ran a job, you could hear the processing flow. The disks would spin louder, or they would quiet down. You knew when something was going on that took more storage, and if it went on for some time, chances are there would be an error of some sort in the code. As the main CPU would run longer, the ventilator fans would come on to cool the work in that part of the machine.

While the history of the mainframe could be a book by itself, one thing that the mainframe excelled at was error messages.

Not to say that the error messages told you specifically what was wrong; they just never lied.

I sat at the master console, learning the IPL procedure. My teacher was over my shoulder, showing me how to interpret each output line that slowly scrolled across the vintage green terminal. He was already familiar with a few errors he could troubleshoot from memory.

The one thing I learned from those sessions of getting the machine up and running was related to troubleshooting. My teacher did not need to know the meaning of every error message. However, each error message contained a code. It would tell you the type of subsystem that was having an error, the number of the error, and a brief description.

One error often leads to a dozen more, so you would have to scroll through the console logs to find the first one or two error messages.

As much as these error codes may have been cryptic, there were answers in the manuals.

I learned how to interpret the codes, find the manual associated with each code, and then find the error message, which usually included a longer explanation of what could cause that error and a recommended fix.

These manuals were so well written that even a fifteen-year-old could read the messages and understand them sufficiently to know how to solve the problems. That is not to say the solution was easy every time I encountered an error. There were plenty of times when reading an error message's details would reference another manual, and so on. Sometimes, it was like pulling a thread. Specific error messages had bridges to other error messages and procedures to address and solve the problem.

However, the lesson stuck. Carefully read the error message, look up the meaning behind the associated codes, and do the same for all the error messages surrounding the first one.

As the behemoth asked for a particular input, the teacher patiently explained the meaning of each request. In the first few weeks, I mastered the IPL procedure.

Since this was an early mainframe, it still used punched cards as input.[7]

It was here that I learned about the history of punched cards. It is a fascinating story, which I have referenced in the footnotes. The nutshell story from my perspective is that as the demand for tapestries and cloth increased in the late 1700s and early 1800s, people searched for ways to

---

[7] https://en.wikipedia.org/wiki/Punched_card

make these items in an automated manner. Joseph Jacquard invented a machine that could be attached to a loom where the patterns the loom would produce could be "programmed," and the machine would make a tapestry that conformed to the design.[8] Creating the correct pattern on the card became the essential step rather than the manual control of the machine that produced the product.

The idea of these replaceable, easily customizable, quickly designed punched cards inspired Charles Babbage in the design of his analytical engine.[9]

This loom was something with which I was already physically familiar. I had done weaving in some of the classes I had taken. This card punch thing as a machine control method made sense. As we jumped from mainframes over to our Tandy machines, then the Apple][s' that compressed the power of that mainframe into a small box on a desk, hardware manufacturing methods had increased in efficiency to make things smaller, and it was demonstrated in our lab. In one room, a single computer. In the other room, there were dozens of computers. Architecturally similar, but physically smaller.

One of my first epiphanies was that I could build on something I knew to learn how something new worked. I will not say my hardware and software classes became easy

---

[8] https://en.wikipedia.org/wiki/Jacquard_machine

[9] https://en.wikipedia.org/wiki/History_of_computing_hardware#First_general-purpose_computing_device

for me, but everything clicked. I jumped in with both feet and never looked back.

I was like a sponge, learning everything I could. In my senior year, a new teacher took us in a different direction. Instead of focusing most of our work on the mainframe, he pushed us towards smaller systems and newer programming languages. We began learning some newer programming languages. He introduced us to dBase.[10] We built a date-matching application for a fundraiser in 1986. Many years later, I was reminded of this little project when I learned about data science.

For our senior project, we built an application to manage students, classes, and teachers. The application would define a teacher for a class, assign students to the class, then assign them to the next class, and assign the various classrooms they need to go to, depending on their schedule.

As a group project, we divided it among the three top students. I created all the data structures and set up how to read and write the data. Another student made the screens for data input, reporting, and selection. A third created all the logic for student promotions.

So, at seventeen years old, I was already a back-end database developer, at least in dBase III.

---

[10] https://en.wikipedia.org/wiki/DBase

The Marine Corps

Soon after high school graduation and a semester of college, I joined the Marine Corps.

I wanted to serve my country and use and expand my knowledge about computer technology. After recruit training, I graduated with high honors from my programming school. The Marine Corps decided the best place for me was as a mainframe database administrator in Quantico, Virginia.

I was absorbing everything, learning from anyone who would answer my questions. But I will never forget the day my badge opened the door to the computer room unescorted.

For a moment, I was that grade school kid staring in wonder at the equipment that surrounded me, as if I had been transported through the window of that room at the Johnson Space Center into this room. Only this time, I knew what most of the equipment in that room did and how it worked.

Over time, my responsibilities increased. We needed to upgrade our leading database software, which was running all the Marine Corps' business applications, from version 4 to version 5. Since I was new, my boss made me learn everything I could about ADABAS version 5.

I installed the older version. I upgraded, tested, verified, and performed downgrades, backups, restores, migrations, and every utility that needed to run in production. The systems team I worked on had a separate mainframe from the production machine, making it easy to experiment, test, learn, and simulate things we needed to do.

I became our expert on ADABAS version 5. I upgraded all our production databases based at Quantico from ADABAS version 4 to 5 and wrote procedures that were sent to the rest of the Marine Corps mainframe sites. I taught the other DBAs the migration procedures and supported them in their efforts to upgrade the other mainframe sites that supported the Marine Corps mission.

And then, on the second of August 1990, the world changed when Iraq invaded Kuwait.

The buildup of American resources called Operation Desert Shield in Saudi Arabia included a large group of Marines. The Marine Corps doctrine for a deployment required a "local" mainframe that would handle all the data associated with ordering supplies, managing human resources (promotions, medals, casualties), and payroll. Based on the requirements given by command, the number of Marine resources in theater was much greater than the existing system's capabilities. Overall, the total number of Marines deployed to Desert Shield/Storm was between 45,000 and 90,000 in round numbers. The old system could not scale to support this large number in theater. We could process things, but it was slow.

Because of my expertise with ADABAS version 5, I was put on a team of twelve Marines who were tapped to replace the existing system with a new one. Our goal was for the team in theater to run backups on the old system, walk the tapes over to the devices attached to the new system, run a restore job, and be up and running. Sounds like an easy process.

You can think of a mainframe from this period as an older car fresh off the manufacturing line—no hoses, tubes, or wires connecting any parts. The Mainframe systems programmers (which is what I was at the time with a specialty in databases) must tell the mainframe what devices are connected, how to communicate with these devices, and what other things it needs to do to operate.

Also, the machine that was going to be deployed was not available. That machine was being put together at a different site in a cargo container that would make it mobile. Once we were ready, we would take all our tapes, travel to where the machine was, and build it out. In the meantime, we had to create a virtual mainframe to work on.

How did we do that?

A virtual mainframe in the early 1990s?

As an aside, VMWare, one of the earliest tools for running virtual machines, was launched in 1998.

Since the systems team had our mainframe for testing and research, we used it. I would back up the disk devices at the end of the official working day, then restore the tapes from the system build-out we were doing. Everyone would prepare what they needed to do, and then, closer to midnight, I would back up the "new" system to tapes. Restore the "old" system from the tapes I had used to backup earlier in the afternoon.

We created a virtual mainframe.

In a world with no GIT, no JIRA, and no Agile.

Agile was made up in 2001.

Jira was released in 2002.

Git was invented in 2005.

After writing procedures, programs, and documentation, we had everything put together for us to build out this machine. In mid-January, the team traveled from Northern Virginia to where the actual physical machine was and began our work.

We did our work and wrapped up the cargo container that held the result of the project. Eight members of the team went to Saudi Arabia. The other four of us returned to Quantico to support things remotely.

On 17 January 1991, Operation Desert Shield became Operation Desert Storm.

The cargo container flew to its destination. The on-site team received it and got to work with the migration.

The migration happened with **ZERO** data loss. I wish some of the projects I participated in later could say the same. I do not take full credit for this success. We worked as a team. Those of us doing the build-out of the machine, the Marines taking the container in theater, those receiving it, and then doing the necessary steps to do the migration made this happen. I did my part, and our team was successful.

Most of the Marines we were supporting did not even realize we did a mainframe upgrade in a war-theater.

Watching the news and knowing that every warfighter deployed to Saudi Arabia and through to the counter-invasion of Kuwait depended on the systems we had deployed made me realize that every bit of data we were working with represented a real, living, breathing person.

Data represents people!

Today, we think of data as just ones and zeros residing on some computer in the cloud. During that time, data represented my brothers and sisters working and fighting for a better future for people halfway around the world.

I have always remembered the lesson that data represents people.

Operation Desert Storm was over quickly, and soon, my time in the Marines ended.

Professional life

"To develop a complete mind: Study the science of art; Study the art of science. Learn how to see. Realize that everything connects to everything else." - Leonardo da Vinci

Remember my comment about Mainframes being considered a trade technology and not cutting-edge in the late 1980s'?

After I separated from active duty, I did work on mainframe systems for a while. However, the winds of change made it clear that there was only a limited future working with mainframes. As one of my favorite characters in fiction said: "So, I went to the library" (Hermione Granger). I read book after book on personal computers. I learned as I went working on non-mainframe systems.

Life happens, and time goes on through various jobs, locations, ups and downs, projects, certifications, and implementations.

I even did some side consulting, training, and startup work. Eventually, I worked my way up to being a Data Architect. I could design data structures and physical machine layouts, explain how the databases communicated with the applications, and apply various use cases for an application database versus an enrichment platform. I had truly accomplished something.

However, only some people within the enterprises I worked with understood what I was doing. I realize now that when most people think of work done with computers, they think of system administrators or application developers. The Data People of the world are overlooked more often than is appreciated.

The data structures, transformation routines, and data movement processes that my team or I would create would go into some presentation layer or Excel extract, where a business analyst would do a little math and draw some pictures with the data, and suddenly, they would be considered genius.

I realized they were taking credit for most of the work my team and I were doing. Realizing there was a gap in my knowledge that prevented me from turning the data structures I worked with into valuable knowledge products, I began researching how to become a Data Scientist.

Data science was growing in popularity. It seemed as if new data science schools were popping up every day. I found one that was completely online and went to work.

The mathematical epiphany

"Philosophy is written in this grand book, the universe, which stands continually open to our gaze. But the book cannot be understood unless one first learns to comprehend the language and read the letters in which it is composed. It is written in the language of mathematics, and its characters are triangles, circles, and other geometric figures" - Galileo

I had to relearn mathematics from the ground up. In my religious education, teachers taught just enough math to enable a person to balance a checkbook—nothing more precise than that. The business analysts and these new people I was speaking with, who were called data scientists, spoke in a different language. They were using terms I thought I was familiar with, but they had a different meaning for some of the terms I thought I understood.

I started from the beginning. I read every math book I could, did the exercises, and thought about how to apply this knowledge to my daily work. Just as I had been a sponge in learning the mechanics of working with computers, I dove in with everything I could in learning mathematics.

After completing the fundamentals—algebra, geometry, statistics, trigonometry, calculus, and probability—I began exploring the more sophisticated areas of mathematics— things like Topology, Graph Theory, Category Theory, and others. These topics initially fascinated me, but I needed a practical use case to work with these advanced mathematical tools. Over time, as I learned to apply what I had learned, I began to see things I thought I understood in a new light.

There were many anecdotal stories of the great minds of mathematics. Some are fascinating, and some are more than likely apocryphal.

There was one story that tied together my background in data organization and analytical insights.

The apocryphal story goes like this: When Carl Frederick Gauss[11] was a boy, his teacher wanted a bit of a break. So, the teacher assigned the students the task of adding up all numbers from one through one hundred. After just a few minutes, the boy walked up to the desk with the answer. Astonished, the teacher verified that the answer was correct.

---

[11] https://en.wikipedia.org/wiki/Carl_Friedrich_Gauss

The specifics of this story have yet to be discovered, with some historians saying it is a fabrication and others claiming it to be true. I will assume the story is accurate and, while playing devil's advocate, show one way the young Gauss could have produced the answer.

Assume for a moment that you need to complete this task. Traditionally, the way many teachers explain addition is in the following manner:

$$\begin{array}{r} 1 \\ +1 \\ \hline 2 \end{array}$$

Following this approach, a student may begin writing a column of numbers as such:

$$\begin{array}{r} 1 \\ +2 \\ +3 \\ +4 \\ \hline \end{array}$$

And so on. This could take some time just to write everything down. I suspect the teacher also knew this and was hoping the children would work quietly while they wrote everything down.

What if the way the problem is written changes how you produce the answer? What if, instead of doing it vertically, you broke it up into pieces and wrote it down horizontally? Like this:

1	2	3	4	5	6	7	8	9	10	11
100	99	98	97	96	95	94	93	92	91	90
101	101	101	101	101	101	101	101	101	101	101

Suddenly, this looks like a different problem. When the set of numbers one through fifty is added to one hundred through fifty-one, they each sum to 101.

Since there are fifty instances of this addition, the answer to the summary problem becomes:

101X50

Which is 5050.

Let us look at that expression to make this approach more generic and valuable for summarizing any set of numbers.

(101X50) = 5050

Knowing that we have a total of 100 numbers, what would happen if we change the expression slightly:

(101X100)/2= 5050

Hmm, I see something that looks like a pattern. Could we then say that the sum of any set of numbers from 1 through N is (N*(N+1))/2?

Here is how a mathematician might write out the above proof using algebra.

We will set n = 10 in this case to keep it on one page.

We know that there will be two equations.

One forward:

T = 1 + 2 + 3 + 4 + 5 + (n-4) + (n-3) + (n-2) + (n-1) + n

And one backward:

T = n + (n-1) + (n-2) + (n-3) + (n-4) + 5 + 4 + 3 + 2 + 1

Adding these together, we have:

T = 1 + 2 + 3 + 4 + 5 + (n-4) + (n-3) + (n-2) + (n-1) + n

+   <u>T = n   + (n-1) + (n-2) + (n-3) + (n-4) + 5 + 4 + 3 +</u>
2 + 1

2T = (n+1)+(n+1) + (n+1) + (n+1) + (n+1) + (n+1) + (n+1) + (n+1) + (n+1) + (n+1)

Since there are **n** copies of **(n+1)**, this translates to:

2T = n(n+1)

The actual total would then be:

T = n(n+1)/2

By substituting 10 for n, the answer is 10(11)/2 = 55.

The original Gauss problems answer becomes 100(101)/2 = 5050

Q.E.D. [12]

Looking at things from this perspective was a momentous moment for me. Data structures could assist in finding a solution to a problem. I had known this empirically through my experience, but here is a proper mathematical

---

[12] https://en.wikipedia.org/wiki/Q.E.D.

definition showing that the data arrangement in a specific way created a shortcut to finding a solution.

This manuscript not only shows the journey I took to learn more advanced mathematics, but also how I applied this advanced mathematics to the study of data structures.

It was convoluted to uncover the relationship between these mathematical concepts and the data structures I understood. In this work, I have made this much more straightforward.

The concept to which I am referring is the concept of data modeling.

Data modeling

"There were 5 exabytes of information created between the dawn of civilization through 2003, but that much information is now created every two days." - Eric Schmidt

Data modeling is the process of creating a conceptual representation of data structures, relationships, and rules within an organization's information ecosystem. It defines and organizes data assets to facilitate efficient storage, retrieval, and manipulation of data.

Data modeling helps in understanding data requirements, designing databases, and building applications or analytical systems.

There are many schools of thought on data modeling. From what I have gathered while working with a large variety of people, the type of data modeling that is most prevalent in academia is application design.

Application

An application is what is running when you sign on to a website or log in to a software system to work. Excel is an application. The bank's website is an application. A video game is an application. Every valuable application creates, reads, updates, and deletes (possibly) data that must be saved for some time. There are legal requirements related to data storage in every country. In the United States, one important rule is that financial data must be available for seven years.

The word 'available' can have multiple interpretations, and I have seen a variety of ways to interpret this word over time. This diversity in interpretation underscores the need for professionals in the field to be open-minded and adaptable, ready to understand and accommodate different perspectives.

Data modeling is important in application design for:

- **Structure and organization**: Data modeling provides a blueprint for organizing data within an application. It helps define the structure of the database, specifying tables, attributes, and relationships. This ensures data consistency and integrity, making it easier to retrieve and manipulate data efficiently.

- **Data integrity and validation:** Data modeling is instrumental in enforcing data constraints and validation rules. Data modeling ensures that data entered into the application meets the required standards and integrity rules by specifying data types, primary and foreign key relationships, and constraints. This robust system instills a sense of security and confidence in the data management process.

- **System performance:** Efficient data modeling improves application performance. Adequately designed data models optimize data retrieval, storage, and processing. Based on the data model, indexes and query optimizations can be implemented, leading to faster response times and a better overall user experience.

Note that the application database usually performs better when the volume of data is smaller. Many tables in an application database will reach a plateau and grow slowly over time. The more essential tables tend to grow rapidly, negatively affecting performance over time.

This is one of the many reasons the data community has devised the solution of offloading data from the primary application to a secondary location. This data can be adapted and used in ways that extend beyond the application's original design and intended functions.

One mechanism for pulling data from an application to an integration area is Change Data Capture (CDC). This mechanism identifies what data has changed and when it was changed to offload the data to another system. This other system could be a replica, an integration layer, a reporting system, or an enrichment platform.

I will discuss the relationship between an application and its database in the section on economics. This relationship is the same regardless of whether the application is a bespoke application built for an enterprise or a canned suite of software like a business intelligence tool or reporting tool.

Integration

Not every enrichment platform is a data warehouse. Today, there are a variety of buzzword-filled names for an integration layer; the evolution of terms for something that brings data together from a variety of sources to make it easy to summarize and aggregate will never end. "Enrichment platform" has become a catch-all phrase for many data integration and management tools. While some enrichment platforms may have features like a data warehouse, they are not necessarily the same thing.

Data modeling is of paramount importance in the integration use case due to the following reasons:

- Data is often sourced from multiple systems and various data sources. Data modeling provides a consistent and unified view of the data, making integrating and analyzing information from different sources easier.

- Data modeling helps establish standardized definitions, formats, and rules for data elements. It ensures that data is consistent, accurate, and of high quality, enabling reliable analysis and decision-making.

- Data modeling considers future growth and changes in data requirements. It enables the design of scalable data structures and allows for modifications or additions to the data model as new information becomes available or business needs evolve.

When combining data from various applications, some of which may be off-the-shelf software applications, the data organization, data types, quality, consistency, and veracity may all conform to different standards depending on the requirements of the individual applications.

When bringing data together into an integrated whole, we must understand how data in one system relates to data in another system. For example, the column "FullName" from one system may be conceptually consistent with the combination of the columns "First-name," "Middle-name," and "Last-name" in another system. How confident are you that if we combine the three columns from system two into a single column, that result will 100% match the one column from system one on the first try?

Presentation

Data modeling enables the creation of reusable, complex analytical models. It defines relationships between data entities, hierarchies, and aggregations that are crucial for performing advanced analytics and generating meaningful reports.

Note that the goals of data modeling for application design and analytical data warehousing have very different objectives. More on this later.

Data modeling provides structure, integrity, and performance optimizations for applications while also facilitating data integration, consistency, and advanced analysis in data warehousing scenarios. Its importance cannot be overstated in ensuring the efficiency and effectiveness of data-driven applications and decision-making processes. In my journey, I learned much more about the mathematics behind data modeling than I even thought existed.

Our journey

"Enjoy the journey and try to get better every day. And don't lose the passion and the love for what you do." - Nadia Comaneci

My journey to tie these things together was like wandering in the wilderness, looking for interesting flowers.

I will start with set theory and logic and then show how relational algebra and calculus work as a foundation. Once we have thus established our approach, we can see how more advanced mathematics can be applied to the structures we will be studying.

We must understand set theory, functions, and logic in order to write SQL. Some of the more advanced topics I will discuss are optional for understanding SQL and data structures. Yet, you need to understand the advanced concepts or pay the opportunity costs of doing things inefficiently.

Most books on set theory remind me of the Tom and Jerry cartoon where Tom needs to have the waltz playing on the piano for Jerry to dance. He finds a book that says how to play the waltz in six easy lessons by Johann Strauss. He goes through each of the lessons, and at the end of the book, he throws it away and plays as if he were an expert.

Set theory instruction gives a few definitions of some hieroglyphs, and within a few pages, everything is communicated in said hieroglyphs.

In introducing set theory, I aim to use it as a launching pad for some of the more advanced mathematics and relational theory implemented conceptually by most RDBMS (Relational Database Management System).

My experience in the industry leads me to believe that, among the people with whom I have worked, most developers' educational curricula provide extraordinarily little exposure to set theory.

As a database administrator, I could promptly identify an individual's lack of comprehension regarding set theory when they excessively employ SQL cursors or stored procedures for various tasks. This approach indicates that the individual is performing single-threaded operations, disregarding the robust capabilities offered by a relational database.

It's important to acknowledge that there may be instances where performance constraints hinder the implementation of optimal practices. If the performance constraints of your existing system prevent you from doing things the right way, you need to fire your management team and get someone in charge who understands the constraints provided to the data team.

Do not get me wrong. Like any tool, these things have their place, but if your only tool is a hammer, every problem becomes a nail.

Not everything is a nail.

Set theory has an inbred cousin, logic. Although you can apply logical rules away from set theory, set theory requires logical rules.

Set theory is a group of objects. The term "object" is vague. That is because as a set is defined, the objects contained in the set are defined through the doctrines of logic.

These doctrines must be studied, at the very least in principle, to understand how they apply to sets.

I intend to examine these doctrines and translate "natural language" into the hieroglyphics I mentioned before.

Using this foundation, we can revisit the definition of relational theory as defined by Date and Codd and expand it further to create new mathematical objects used by data scientists, business analysts, and other knowledge workers in their daily lives. The synthesis I will discuss further is the synthesis of the areas of data science, business analysis, and application performance. These different things can be improved by using the same data structures but for various purposes.

We must go through the definition steps to ensure these constructs are defined clearly for later use. If we do not define them clearly in the language of mathematics, then we cannot leverage the mathematical tools that various mathematicians have independently developed throughout the world.

Leveraging these other tools will allow us to learn new things about the structures we use, independent of their data.

The structures themselves have meanings that can provide self-referential (foreshadowing) contextual information about the data stored within our application databases and enrichment platforms.

In addition to this contextual information, the structures themselves give hints on how to transform data from the SQL (relational) to the NoSQL (non-relational world) and vice-versa. And from one type of relational system (application) to a different kind of relational system (analytical)

So, for anyone doing data engineering, these mathematical principles explain not only why you are performing some sort of transformation but also why you **must** form a specific transformation.

TWO

Troubleshooting

"The more you sweat in training, the less you bleed in combat."
- Richard Marcinko, Rogue Warrior

Troubleshooting is the art of ignoring the wrong and focusing on the right. It involves figuring out why the actual thing that is happening is different from the expected thing that should be happening. I have taken pride in tackling and solving intricate problems throughout my career. Occasionally, a particularly challenging issue would emerge, requiring the combined expertise of an entire team.

Troubleshooting is a nuanced and often misunderstood process. It is not merely about fixing what is broken; it is an art form that hinges on distinguishing between what is relevant and what is not. This process involves a careful, systematic approach to identifying and solving problems. It requires a blend of knowledge, experience, experimentation, and intuition to identify the root causes of issues and address them effectively.

At its core, troubleshooting is about focusing on the right things. This type of focus means being able to ignore distractions or misleading symptoms that might lead you down a rabbit hole of irrelevant fixes. It is about recognizing patterns, understanding how systems work, and knowing which components will fail. This ability to focus is not innate but developed through experience and training.

Troubleshooting requires training. Training provides the foundational knowledge and skills necessary to understand how a system or technology operates. Without this background, troubleshooting can be like finding your way in a dark room. You may eventually stumble upon the solution, but the process will be inefficient and fraught with errors.

If you've yet to receive training on a specific piece of technology, why are you the one attempting to troubleshoot it? Your familiarity with the technology directly impacts your ability to troubleshoot effectively. As a novice, you may overlook common issues or misinterpret what you observe. In contrast, a deep understanding of the technology allows for quicker and more accurate problem diagnosis.

What level of familiarity with the technology is ideal? The answer depends on the complexity of the technology and your role in using or maintaining it. For example, a deep, nuanced understanding of that system is essential if you are responsible for managing a complex IT system. On the other hand, if you are an end user of a software application, a basic understanding might be sufficient for minor troubleshooting, with experts tackling the more complex issues.

If you have been using a technology for a significant period, say a year or more, and still consider yourself a novice, you must improve your foundational knowledge. In such cases, it is advisable to start over with the fundamentals. This means returning to the basics: reading the documentation, tutorials, and other learning materials. It is about resetting your knowledge and filling in the gaps that have developed over time. This re-education can provide new insights into problems you have been facing and equip you with more effective troubleshooting strategies. The lesson about re-educating yourself on things you think you know was hard for me to learn. Do not be afraid to return to the fundamentals of something you think you understand.

The troubleshooting process should involve constant self-reflection. Asking yourself why you are doing a particular thing is crucial. This introspection helps to avoid automatic or habitual actions that may not be appropriate for the current problem. It forces you to consider whether your approach is based on solid reasoning or simply following a routine that might not be applicable.

Effective troubleshooting involves a systematic approach. It is of paramount importance to follow a structured process to identify and resolve issues. This process often starts with clearly defining the problem.

- What exactly is malfunctioning?
- Are there any error messages or abnormal behaviors?
- What is the typical behavior?

The next step is to gather information. This involves collecting data, including logs, user reports, or direct observations.

After gathering information, the next step is to analyze the data. Your training and experience play a crucial role in this analysis. You need to interpret the information, looking for clues pointing to the problem's root cause. This stage may involve hypothesizing what is wrong and testing those hypotheses.

After identifying the root cause, plan and implement a solution. The solution could involve fixing a bug, replacing a faulty component, or adjusting a configuration. Test and validate the solution to ensure it resolves the issue and does not introduce new problems.

Finally, a crucial aspect of troubleshooting is documentation and learning. After resolving an issue, document what you found, how you fixed it, and any lessons learned. Documentation of the solution helps in case the problem reoccurs and contributes to the collective knowledge of your team or organization.

Troubleshooting is an exercise in patience and persistence. The solution is rarely immediately apparent, and the problem might require prolonged investigation. It is vital to remain methodical and only assume a conclusion based on evidence. Sometimes, stepping back from the problem or consulting with colleagues can provide a fresh perspective that leads to a solution.

In conclusion, troubleshooting is a critical skill that combines knowledge, experience, and a systematic approach. It is about knowing what to focus on and what to ignore, understanding the technology you are working with, and constantly questioning your methods. With the right mindset and approach, troubleshooting can be a gratifying process, offering the satisfaction of solving complex problems and keeping systems running smoothly.

For example, one of the most well-thought-out projects in the history of humanity was the moon landings.

In early 1969, Gene Kranz assembled his team for the descent phase of Apollo 11. In a few short months, they were to prepare their landing plan, establish their GO/NO GO mission rules, test all aspects of the plan in the simulators, and execute their mission. Their job was to get the Lunar Module from lunar orbit down to the decision point for Armstrong and Aldrin to attempt the landing.

Steve Bales was one of the engineers selected for the team. Kranz describes Bales as a 26-year-old bespectacled computer whiz kid—one of the first of his kind. He was chosen as the Guidance Officer (GUIDO, pronounced "guy-doe") for the descent phase. GUIDO is responsible for the navigation and computer software of the spacecraft, in this case, the Lunar Module. Bales' job was to produce his set of mission rules for the descent phase.

Kranz's team got their time on the simulators just eight weeks before the landing attempt. Amazingly, they only had 11 days of simulator time: seven days with the crew and four days with math models and simulated astronauts. But as any member of NASA would tell you, these are some of the longest days of your life.

The legendary hell inflicted on mission controllers and astronauts during the simulations came compliments of the instructors and their lead, the Simulation Supervisor (SimSup). Dick Koos, described as a quiet young academic by Kranz, was the SimSup for the descent phase training. Koos had a background with the U.S. Army in computer guidance for ground-to-air missiles and NASA recruited him in 1960 to work in their Simulation Group.

The first few days of simulator time for Kranz' team were spent working out their landing plan and becoming familiar with all of the decision points. After that break-in period, they really got down to work running training scenarios. Kranz described Koos' training sessions "like a rapier, cutting so cleanly that you did not know you were bleeding until long after the thrust."

Eventually, Kranz and his team worked out the kinks and became increasingly successful at getting the astronauts to their decision point for landing.

On July 5, 1969, the team had their final simulator run. An unwritten tradition had formed over these early years of the space program for the SimSup to let their students end on a high note by offering up a softball scenario (a test that is not complicated in any way). However, Koos had a different plan for Kranz's team.

On the final run, Koos had his team load up a brand-new scenario. He wanted to find out how much Kranz's team knew about computer program alarms. Three minutes into the scenario, Koos' team threw a program alarm. Responsible for the Lunar Module computer, Bales was busy ensuring he was getting the guidance data right when his display began showing a 1201 alarm code, indicating a computer restart. The Lunar Module pilot in the simulator also saw the alarm code and didn't know what to do with it.

Bales quickly referenced the Lunar Module software handbook and read that the code meant the computer was overloaded and could not complete all of its jobs in time. Bales had not written a single mission rule regarding program alarms, so he had yet to learn how to proceed.

After conferring with a back-room software colleague, Bales was told the 1201 was a BAILOUT alarm in the high stakes of a lunar landing, where every second counts. Bales was rapidly getting behind the power curve. Bales made the call to ABORT the landing.

In the after-action review, Koos evaluated the team's performance, concluding with the stabbing revelation that "THIS WAS NOT AN ABORT. YOU SHOULD HAVE CONTINUED THE LANDING."

According to Kranz, Koos continued, "If guidance was working, the control jets firing, and the crew displays updating, all of the mission-critical tasks [for the computer] were getting done."

Frustrated by his performance, Bales pulled a team together and, on July 11, 1969, modified an already extensive list of reasons to abort a lunar landing to include the program alarms. He listed all of the alarms that would mandate an abort. Alarms 1201 and 1202 were not on that list.

Nine days later, on July 20, 1969, during Armstrong and Aldrin's descent to the lunar surface, shortly after the landing radar kicked on, Aldrin radios to Mission Control, "Program alarm. It's a 1202."

Charlie Duke, CAPCOM, repeats in the control room, "It's a 1202 alarm," followed a little later with, "It's the same one we had in training."

Kranz writes, "These were the same exact alarms that brought us to the wrong conclusion, an abort command, in the final training run when SimSup won the last round. This time we won't be stampeded."

Bales says, "We're Go on that alarm. If it doesn't recur, we are Go."

A backroom controller was inadvertently heard saying, "This is just like the simulation."

A short while later, they see another program alarm. Aldrin calls, "Same alarm, and it appears to come up when we have [a display active that monitors landing site range and altitude]."

Bales responds quickly, "We are Go. Tell him we will monitor his altitude data. I think that is why he is getting the alarm."

Kranz writes, "I mentally thank SimSup for the final training run on program alarms." Kranz successfully arrives at the decision point of their checklist to hand over control to Armstrong and Aldrin for the final phase of the landing. All of his rule criteria had been met.

This is the point in the story where the well-known archival footage picks up. No doubt you've seen this footage and heard the dialog. If you haven't, you will have ample opportunity as we come up on the 50th anniversary of the moon landing. In this footage, you will hear Aldrin call out another 1201 alarm at 3,000 feet and a 1202 alarm at 1,400 feet.

The rest, as they say, is history.

Before leaving for the press conference, Kranz writes, "I walk into the simulation control room to thank Koos and the training team. The instructors are unbelieving that the last problem given us in training is the one big problem during the landing."

On August 13, 1969, at a presidential dinner in Los Angeles, Steve Bales, the software whiz kid who learned his lesson thanks to crafty instructors, high-fidelity simulators, and adequate training, accepted the Medal of Freedom on behalf of the entire Apollo 11 flight operations team.[13]

The previous story from *Failure is Not an Option* is one of the best examples of troubleshooting problems based on training.

Troubleshooting technology problems can be frustrating but essential to resolving issues and ensuring your devices and systems work as intended.

---

[13] Failure is not an option: Mission control from Mercury to Apollo 13 and beyond. New York: Simon & Schuster Paperbacks.

While technology issues are sometimes related to hardware, they are more often related to software. This software could be source code for a scripting language, a compiled language, or configuration files that are used as input to another process.

The following is a crucial non-exclusive list of steps to assist in troubleshooting:

- **Identify the problem:** Start by pinpointing the specific issue you are facing. Is it related to hardware (physical components) or software (programs and applications)? If it is software, what component is breaking? Is it networking, memory, CPU, Storage, configuration, or application related? Understanding the nature of the problem will help you narrow down the troubleshooting process. Just identifying the actual problem can take more time than expected. There are times when it appears you have identified the problem, but when you make a change, the problem persists. At this point, you still need to identify the problem. One of my favorite techniques for determining the problem is to make a change you "know" is not related to the problem.

- **Make other changes not related to the issue:** Make one change you are confident has nothing to do with the error you received. If making this change causes an unexpected error, combining the information gained from this change with the original error may point you in the right direction.

- **Reproduce the issue:** Try replicating the problem in another environment. This can help you determine if the issue is intermittent or consistent and provide additional information for troubleshooting. When working with code, create a new copy of the code that is failing in a new folder or environment. Is it the code or the environment?

- **Check for user errors:** Sometimes, the issue may be due to user error. Ensure you use the technology correctly by referring to user manuals or online resources. Double-check settings, connections, and inputs. Having made more user errors than I care to admit, the probability that you did something stupid is highest of all.

- **Restart/Reboot:** A simple reboot can often resolve many memory-related problems. Restart the affected device or application and see if the issue persists. This helps clear temporary glitches and conflicts. You may need to reboot servers that are going haywire. In the case of containers, restart the container or download the base image and start over again.

- **Use online resources:** The internet is a valuable tool for troubleshooting. Search for the specific error message or problem description online. Forums, community websites, and official support pages may have solutions or workarounds. Again, to use online resources, you must understand the problem. Applying advice from Stack Overflow when you need more clarity on precisely the problem you are facing will cause more issues. The footnote is a reference for asking intelligent questions.[14]

- **Consult documentation**: Read the documentation, help guides, and manuals for your technology or software. These resources often contain troubleshooting steps and tips. If necessary, walk away from the problem and then come back and reread it.

- **Try basic fixes**: Start with the simplest and most common solutions, such as restarting the device or application. Sometimes, a simple reboot can resolve many issues.

- **Update software and firmware**: Ensure your operating system, software applications, and device firmware are current. Manufacturers often release updates to address bugs and improve functionality. If the updates have not been applied for some time, consult the manufacturer for suggestions on updating from older versions.

- **Check connectivity**: For devices that rely on internet connectivity, ensure you have a stable internet connection. Restart your modem/router if necessary. If using Wi-Fi, check signal strength and try moving closer to the router.

---

[14] https://github.com/selfteaching/How-To-Ask-Questions-The-Smart-Way

- **Inspect hardware connections**: For hardware issues, check all physical connections. This includes power cables, USB/HDMI cables, and any other relevant connections. Loose or damaged cables can lead to problems.

- **Run diagnostic tools**: Many devices and operating systems have built-in diagnostic tools. Utilize these tools to identify and fix issues automatically. For example, Windows has the built-in "Troubleshoot" feature.

- **Check for error messages**: Pay attention to any error messages or notifications you receive. These messages often contain valuable information about the problem and viable solutions.

- **Isolate the issue**: If you have multiple devices connected, try to isolate the problem. Disconnect or turn off devices one by one to see if the issue is related to a specific component.

- **Search online resources**: Use search engines, manufacturer websites, and user forums to find solutions to your problem. Others may have encountered and resolved the same issue.

- **Backup data**: If you suspect a significant issue that could lead to data loss, backup your important files and data before attempting any significant fixes.

- **Factory reset**: If all else fails and you are dealing with a persistent software issue, consider a factory reset. This should be a last resort, as it will erase all data and settings on the device. Make sure to back up important data before proceeding.

- **Contact customer support**: If you cannot resolve the issue on your own, contact the manufacturer's customer support. They can provide guidance, troubleshoot remotely, or arrange for repairs or replacements.

- **Seek professional help**: If you are dealing with complex hardware problems or need to be more comfortable with DIY repairs, consult a professional technician or service center.

Remember that troubleshooting may require patience and persistence. It is essential to approach the process systematically, ruling out potential causes one by one until you find the solution to your technology problem.

Keep a record

Document the steps you have taken and their outcomes throughout the troubleshooting process. This can be useful if you need to seek assistance or if the problem reoccurs.

Rule of three

Once you appear to have a fix, test a typical scenario three times. Why three times? The more tests you run, the higher your level of significance and confidence.

What are the odds that something broke will work after making a change and trying again?

Perhaps it is 50% or one possible positive outcome and one possible negative outcome. Two possible outcomes and one actual outcome.

Now, do the same thing again without making any changes. Two tries of four possible outcomes, again 50% = 50%.

Now, test it once more, and what happens?

The math starts to do interesting things for you.

With only two possible outcomes, and three attempts, that becomes a total of eight outcomes. If it works the third time, what are the probabilities that you have the right solution?

If you do three tests, each with only two possible outcomes, and each test works, the odds become 62.5% that you are right.

The more tests you run, the odds continue to increase in your favor that you have found the correct solution.

Remember that patience and a systematic approach are key when troubleshooting technology problems. By following these techniques, you can increase your chances of effectively resolving issues and maintaining the reliability of your technology.

THREE

Synthesis

"The beauty of mathematics only shows itself to more patient followers." - Maryam Mirzakhani

Knowledge evolves. One person can look at something and say, this is wood, canvas, and some white, blue, orange, and red paint. Another person can look at the same thing and say this appears to be a young woman sitting on a bed contemplating her life. A third person could say this is the painting *Surrender Your Heart* by Pino Daeni. Everyone can be correct. The synthesis of all their thoughts comes together in a single painting.

Synthesis is all about bringing things together.

Synthesis is everywhere, from science to music. In science, synthesis is cooking up new compounds in a lab. In music, it is mixing beats and creating new songs. Synthesis is more comprehensive than science and music. It is the superpower of bringing different things together unexpectedly and making something new and unique.

The concept of synthesis exhibits remarkable manifestation in the technological realm. Consider the internet, initially conceptualized as a scientific communication medium. It has evolved into a ubiquitous platform facilitating a global exchange of information, commerce, and entertainment. It serves scientists sharing research findings, entrepreneurs conducting business transactions, and artists highlighting their creations. Each group harnesses the internet, the shared technological infrastructure, to pursue their unique objectives. In this context, the internet acts as a standard tool that bridges the gap between diverse fields, enabling them to thrive in their respective domains.

The power of synthesis also extends to the realm of ideas. Philosophers throughout history have synthesized concepts from different schools of thought to develop comprehensive systems of knowledge. Immanuel Kant, for instance, synthesized rationalism and empiricism, two opposing philosophical traditions, to create a new framework for understanding learning and reality. Similarly, in the field of psychology, Carl Jung synthesized concepts from various cultures and mythologies to develop his theory of the collective unconscious. St. Augustine synthesized the teachings of Plato, Aristotle, and Socrates with the teachings of the church. These examples demonstrate how the synthesis of ideas can lead to the emergence of novel insights and theories.

Synthesis is a multifaceted concept that combines elements to create a unified whole. It finds expression in diverse fields, from technology and science to philosophy and art.

The power of synthesis lies in its ability to bridge conceptual divides through the utilization of shared tools, thereby enabling the achievement of distinct goals. By recognizing the potential of synthesis, we can unlock new possibilities for innovation and discovery, leading to a more interconnected and enriched understanding of our world.

As the digital landscape continues to evolve, organizations face an ever-increasing volume of data. This data deluge presents a significant challenge, as we may need to revise traditional data management approaches to handle large and complex datasets.

In facing the challenge of managing all of this data, one of the most important tools at our disposal is the ability to create data models to assist in managing the data. A data model is a collection of related Data Structures meant to achieve a common goal. There are a few data modeling techniques that are intended to solve a particular problem. We will delve into their significance in more detail in later sections, making you feel their crucial role in subsequent sections.

One key focus in most university classrooms is application data models. These models are designed to underpin the applications we use daily in our interactions with an enterprise. Their practicality and relevance to our everyday interactions highlight their importance. Application data models provide the foundation for the smooth functioning of the applications we rely on, enabling us to interact with enterprise systems effectively.

Dimensional data models, also known as star schemas, are another critical type of data model. These models are specifically designed to support reporting needs with business intelligence tools. They are characterized by their star-like structure, with a central fact table surrounded by multiple-dimension tables. Dimensional data models are optimized for efficient data retrieval and aggregation, making them ideal for reporting and analysis.

The Data Vault methodology takes a unique approach to data modeling. It combines data from multiple application data models, organizes it according to specific principles, and presents a single consolidated view of data from across the enterprise in a central location. The Data Vault methodology emphasizes data integration, historical preservation, and flexibility. It is often used in complex data environments where multiple source systems and data formats coexist.

In the context of organizing our data, the data vault pattern emerges as a valuable solution, providing a scalable and flexible approach to data modeling for integration.

One principle of the data vault pattern is separating raw data from derived data. This separation ensures that the raw data remains intact and immutable, while derived data can be easily manipulated and transformed without affecting the integrity of the source data. This approach offers numerous advantages, including improved data quality, reduced data redundancy, and increased agility in responding to changing business needs.

One key aspect of the data vault pattern is the graph-based architecture. In this architecture, hubs represent stable entities or concepts over time, such as customers, products, or locations. Links, on the other hand, define relationships between hubs. Satellites provide descriptive or contextual data describing the relationship, the business key, or any needed details. This structure provides a logical and intuitive way to organize and manage complex data relationships.

Overall, the data vault pattern provides a powerful and flexible approach to data modeling that is well-suited for handling large and complex datasets. By separating raw data from derived data and utilizing graph-based architecture, organizations can improve data quality, reduce data redundancy, and increase agility in responding to changing business needs.

The synthesis emerges from various ways to use a given data structure.

While I will focus most of this work on data vault, I intend to focus on the fundamentals of data organization. The principles I cover are not limited to data vaults.

FOUR

Set Theory

"A set is a Many that allows itself to be thought of as a One." -
Georg Cantor

Throughout this book, I will cover some of the
fundamentals of various branches of mathematics. If I were
to write an in-depth treatise on each of these branches, this
book would turn into the volume of an encyclopedia.
Nevertheless, it is crucial to understand the fundamentals
of the theories in this book to know how they relate to the
data structures used in most databases worldwide.
Covering the fundamentals I describe here will not make
you an expert; it will simply make you aware of the
essential aspects of the theories as they apply to organizing
and using data.

---

*Knowing how to run efficiently will not
automatically make you a marathon runner.*

In the zeitgeist of the 17th century, the prevailing problem that many people were trying to solve was finding the longitude of a ship at sea.

Latitude and longitude are how we navigate our globe. Latitude is set by the equator, a fixed point. That means, even out at sea, it is simple to gauge your latitude by the length of the day or the position of the sun. But longitude is more dynamic; it moves as the Earth rotates. Every four minutes, longitude shifts one degree. So, determining longitude, especially at sea, was considered a problem as insoluble as finding the fountain of youth or turning lead into gold.

The longitude problem haunted sailors for centuries. Without establishing longitude, ships' captains relied on what they called "dead reckoning," which meant they were guessing and steering the boat with their gut. Ships were forced to stick to the few safe routes everyone knew.

Between 1550 and 1650, one in five ships was lost between Portugal and India. The issue peaked in the 17th century when British imperial conquest and colonialism relied on sea trade. By the end of the century, nearly three hundred ships a year sailed between the British Isles and the West Indies to ply the Jamaica trade. Commodities and cargo, like sugar and cotton, were transported eastward across the Atlantic to meet consumer demand in Europe.

Galileo did some exciting work using Jupiter's four brightest moons. In 1612, he proposed that with sufficiently accurate knowledge of their orbits, one could use their positions as a universal clock, making the determination of longitude possible.

Isaac Newton, born the same year Galileo died, studied Galileo's work. Some translations of his work claim that Newton credited Galileo for some of the background of Newton's first two laws of motion. Along the way to creating his laws of motion, Newton invented the mathematical subject of calculus. Opening the universe via the mechanism of calculus inspired many physicists and mathematicians to study the details of calculus itself.

Incidentally, a carpenter named John Harrison eventually solved the longitude problem.[15]

One of the mathematicians who decided to study the details of calculus was Goerg Cantor.[16] In the 19th century, Cantor wanted to understand the infinities created when performing derivatives or integrals. By studying the sizes of these infinities and grouping them as individual objects, he invented what we now call Naive Set Theory.

Set theory revolutionized the way mathematicians perceive and work with mathematical objects.

Set theory is a fundamental branch of mathematics that serves as the bedrock for various mathematical disciplines, ranging from elementary arithmetic to advanced topics like topology and analysis.

At its core, set theory deals with studying collections or groups of objects, called (funny enough) "sets." In set theory, sets are considered distinct entities characterized

---

[15] https://en.wikipedia.org/wiki/John_Harrison

[16] https://en.wikipedia.org/wiki/Georg_Cantor

solely by their members. This idea of distinct entities is essential.

By definition, a set contains a unique list of elements. These members, known as elements, can be numbers, shapes, functions, or any other mathematical entities. Sets are typically denoted using braces, while their elements appear within the braces separated by commas.

As an example: {1,2,3,4,6,a,b,c,d,e,g,F,X,I,P,L,~,+,=} would be a set of ASCII (American Standard Code for Information Interchange) characters.

Sets can be made up of other sets. Each set within the parent set must conform to the exact overall definition of a set. For example:

{{red,orange,yellow,green,blue,indigo,violet},{1,2,3,4,5,6, 7},{a,b,c,d,e,f,g},{alice,bob,charlie,david,edward,frank,geo rge}}

As with many things when they were first invented or discovered, Georg Cantor's development of set theory, which he used as an attempt to understand infinite sets, needed additional work. As mentioned previously, what he produced is now called "Naive Set theory." His work is a non-formalized theory that uses "natural language" to describe sets and operations on sets. The assumption that any property may be used to form a set without restriction leads to paradoxes. One typical example is Russell's paradox: there is no set consisting of "all sets that do not contain themselves." Thus, consistent systems of naive set theory must include some limitations on the principles that can be used to form sets.

Axiomatic Set Theory was created to avoid the various paradoxes that exposed inconsistencies within the basic theory. It imposes explicit rules and axioms to ensure a consistent foundation for set theory and the rest of mathematics.

The Zermelo-Fraenkel set theory with the Axiom of Choice (ZFC) is the most widely adopted axiomatic set theory. The ZFC axioms provide a rigorous foundation for set theory, including principles like extensionality, pairing, union, power set, infinity, and the axiom of choice. These axioms enable mathematicians to formulate and prove intricate theorems based on valid logical deductions.

Set theory provides a rich framework for studying relationships between sets. Algebraic operations like union, intersection, and complementation allow us to manipulate and combine sets to obtain new sets. Set relations, such as equality, inclusion, and subset, provide fundamental notions for comparing and classifying sets based on their elements.

Set theory serves as a powerful tool for various branches of mathematics, providing a foundation for advanced topics, such as topology, abstract algebra, and mathematical logic. Additionally, set theory is essential in computer science, especially in the fields of databases, formal languages, and computational complexity theory, where sets and their operations play prominent roles. We will spend much of our focus on set theory around its application in databases and working with sets of data.

One of the tools of set theory is set builder notation. It is necessary to construct a set mathematically from a universe of objects precisely. I will use this notation in a few places throughout this work. The Roster Form in the examples is a list of all of the elements of the set called out explicitly. Not all cases of set builder notation can the Roster form be listed for the list would be longer than the text of this manuscript. Here are a few examples with explanations:

Example 1:

Set Builder Notation: $\{x : x \in \mathbb{N}, x < 5\}$

In words: The set of all x such that x is a natural number (positive whole number), and x is less than 5.

Roster Form: $\{1, 2, 3, 4\}$

Example 2:

Set Builder Notation: $\{y : y \in \mathbb{Z}, y \text{ is even}\}$

In words: The set of all y such that y is an integer and y is even.

Roster Form: $\{..., -4, -2, 0, 2, 4, ...\}$

Example 3:

Set Builder Notation: $\{z \mid z \in \mathbb{R}, 0 \leq z \leq 1\}$

In words: The set of all z such that z is a real number and z is between 0 and 1 (inclusive).

Roster Form: $\{.1, .11, .01, ...\}$

Example 4:

Set Builder Notation: {p | p is a prime number less than 10}

In words: The set of all p such that p is a prime number and p is less than 10.

Roster Form: {2, 3, 5, 7}

Example 5:

Set Builder Notation: {v | v is a vowel in the English alphabet}

In words: The set of all v such that v is a vowel in the English alphabet.

Roster Form: {a, e, i, o, u}

Example 6:

Set Builder Notation: {c | c is a primary color in a rainbow}

In words: The set of all c such that c is a color in a rainbow.

Roster Form: {red, orange, yellow, green, blue, indigo, violet}

With its rigorous axiomatic framework, set theory has paved the way for countless mathematical advancements. By formalizing the notion of collections and their properties, set theory has not only facilitated the development of various mathematical disciplines, but has also challenged our understanding of infinity and the logical foundations of mathematics. As mathematicians continue to explore the depths of set theory, its significance and influence will undoubtedly continue to expand, shaping the future of mathematics.

FIVE

Logic

"A problem well-defined is a problem half solved." - John Dewey

At the core of logic lies one of its most fundamental principles: a statement can either be true or false. This binary nature of truth and falsity serves as the foundation for all logical reasoning and analysis. By comparing, contrasting, expanding, and explaining these "things" that are either true or false, logicians seek to understand the nature of truth, validity, and the structure of sound arguments.

In the realm of logic, several key concepts are closely intertwined with the notion of truth and falsity. Soundness, for instance, refers to the logical validity of arguments or statements. A sound argument is one in which the premises necessarily lead to the conclusion, and the truth of the premises guarantees the truth of the conclusion. On the other hand, an unsound argument may have false premises, invalid reasoning, or both, leading to an unreliable conclusion.

Arguments, reasoning, and statements are all essential components of logical analysis. Arguments consist of a set of premises and a conclusion, where the premises intend to support the conclusion. Reasoning, also known as inference, involves drawing conclusions based on evidence or premises. Statements, on the other hand, are declarative sentences such as "it is raining" that can be evaluated as true or false.

Logicians can determine the validity of arguments by examining the relationship between premises and conclusions. A valid argument is one in which the conclusion necessarily follows from the premises, regardless of whether the premises are true or false. In contrast, an invalid argument may have true premises but a false conclusion, or vice versa.

Furthermore, the study of logic encompasses the analysis of logical fallacies, which are errors in reasoning that lead to invalid conclusions. Identifying and understanding these fallacies allows us to evaluate arguments more critically and distinguish between sound and unsound reasoning.

Let's connect these concepts to the three critical aspects of data management: designing databases, writing queries, and evaluating data.

The best book on logic I have ever read is: "The Art of Logic in an Illogical World" by Eugenia Cheng. I cannot recommend her book highly enough.

Like many children, I grew up watching Star Trek reruns. Mr. Spock, the science officer on the U.S.S. Enterprise in the original series, convinced me that the only thing I really needed to study as I got older was the structure of logic. Every chance I got to study logic, I took it. Only I found it dry and dull, nothing like the dynamic subject I had seen on every episode of the series.

One of the things I learned about logic is that while it is a very fundamental tool, its use can vary widely depending on the subject. Logic in philosophy and logic in mathematics relate more closely to cousins than siblings.

Philosophical logic uses natural language to support its arguments. Mathematical logic can also be symbolic, whereas each symbol has an exact definition. And each variable, like p or q, will have a precise meaning. With philosophical logic, there may be a topic to debate. However, with mathematical logic, we define things precisely to manipulate variables with symbols to conclude the various components of the argument.

The word *logic* comes from the Greek word Logos. One of the earliest references to this word was in Aristotle's Rhetoric. From Aristotle's perspective, the Greek concept of logos refers to logic, reason, and rationality. In Aristotle's philosophy, logos is a fundamental principle that governs the rationality and order of the universe. It encompasses both the logical reasoning process and the resulting knowledge or truth.

For Aristotle, the word *logos* represents human beings' capacity to engage in rational thought, critical thinking, and the ability to articulate ideas through language. Logos is how humans can understand the world, make sense of their experiences, and communicate their thoughts effectively. Aristotle believed logos distinguishes humans from other animals, allowing for critical thinking, logical analysis, and knowledge development. Aristotle's logos assume that the evolution of humanity is rational, not emotional. Emotion should not be a part of rational discourse.

Logic is a fundamental tool in understanding the world around us, and the doctrines of logic that follow provide us with systematic approaches to analyzing and assessing arguments and propositions. Like most things, we can break logic down into a few subjects. This is only a broad overview we will return to when we cover the section on retrieving data.

Implicational and conditional logic

Implicational logic, also known as "if-then" logic, focuses on reasoning about implications and relationships between statements. It deals with conditional statements of the form, "If P, then Q." Here, P is the antecedent or premise, and Q is the consequent or conclusion.

> In conditional logic, we examine the logical relationship between the antecedent and the consequent. If the antecedent holds true, it implies that the consequent will also hold true. However, if the antecedent is false, the status of the consequent remains undetermined.

For example:

If it is raining (P), then the ground is wet (Q).

If it is indeed raining (P), we can logically conclude that the ground will be wet (Q). However, if it does not rain, we cannot make any definitive statement about the condition of the ground.

In many programming languages, the implication becomes a command:

```
If i == 1
then do something
```

We can embed the nature of this little bit of code in many places. We will look at some options for using this code when we get to the DML portion of SQL.

Propositional logic

Propositional logic deals with the relationship between propositions, where a proposition is a declarative statement that can be either true or false. It focuses on analyzing compound propositions composed of logical operators such as conjunction (and), disjunction (or), negation (not), implication (if-then), and double implication (if and only if).

> *Propositional logic allows us to assess the validity and truth value of complex statements by breaking them down into more straightforward propositions and applying logical operators.*

For example:

P: The sun is shining.

Q: The sky is blue.

The conjunction (P ∧ Q) combines the two propositions into: "The sun is shining, and the sky is blue."

The disjunction (P ∨ Q) combines the two propositions into: "The sun is shining, or the sky is blue."

The negation (¬P) transforms the proposition into: "The sun is not shining."

First order predicate logic

Predicate logic allows us to reason about relationships between objects, individuals, and properties. It employs quantifiers, such as the universal quantifier (∀) and existential quantifier (∃), to express generalizations and assertions about properties and relationships.

> *Predicates assign properties or attributes to objects, and variables denote objects or individuals within these predicates.*

For example:

Consider the predicate P(x): "x is a human."

Using the universal quantifier, we can state: ∀x P(x), meaning "For all x, x is a human." This expresses the idea that every object x in our domain is a human.

Using the existential quantifier, we can state: ∃x P(x), meaning "There exists an x such that x is a human." This indicates that at least one human is in the domain.

> Predicate logic allows us to reason about classes of objects, relationships, and properties in a more nuanced and expressive manner than propositional logic.

For reasons that will become obvious later, I wanted to use mathematical notation for the data structures I worked with.

As we will see shortly, relational theory is built around predicate logic. This means we can represent a table or relation using Predicate symbols. A table then becomes:

$$P_t(c_1, \ldots, c_n)$$

Where $c_1, \ldots, c_n$ represent the columns in the definition.

These doctrines of logic provide us with powerful tools to analyze statements, reason about relationships, and evaluate the validity and truth of arguments. By applying conditional, propositional, and predicate logic, we can strive to approach the realm of perfect logic.

Six

Functions

In set theory, a function is a fundamental concept that describes the relationship between two sets. It provides a way to assign each element of one set (called the domain) to a unique element in another set (called the codomain or range). This is a sophisticated way of saying that a function transforms or maps the data in one set into the data in another set. In the case of a function that transforms one set into another set, the function is mapping a mathematical object (a set) into a comparable mathematical object (another set). Later, we will cover the mechanism that transforms one mathematical object into a different mathematical object. Hint: It is not a function!

A function is defined by three components: the domain, the codomain, and the rule or mapping that connects the elements of the domain to the elements of the codomain. Let us go through each component in more detail:

- **Domain**: The domain of a function is the set of values or elements from which to choose inputs.

The letter "x" often denotes these values and represents the independent variable. For example, if we define a function f: A → B, then "A" represents the domain.

- **Codomain:** A function's codomain is the set of all possible values to which the function can map its inputs. The letter "y" often denotes these values and represents the dependent variable. For example, if we define a function f: A → B, then "B" represents the codomain.

- **Mapping rule:** The mapping rule describes how each element in the domain is related to an element in the codomain. It specifies the correspondence or relationship between the function's inputs and outputs. We can express it as a formula, equation, table, or graph. For example, a standard representation for a function is $f(x) = 2x$, which maps each element x in the domain to its double in the codomain.

Functions ensure that each domain element is assigned to a unique element in the codomain. In other words, the mapping has no repeat assignments or ambiguities. If two different domain elements are assigned to the same element in the codomain, then it would violate the definition of a single-value function.

We can represent functions using set notation. The function can be thought of as a subset of the Cartesian product of the domain and the codomain. For example, if f: A → B, then the function can be represented as a set of ordered pairs $\{(a, b) \mid a \in A \text{ and } b \in B\}$.

Overall, functions in set theory provide a formal way to describe relationships between sets by mapping elements from one set to another, ensuring uniqueness and coherence in the process. They are essential tools used in various areas of mathematics and have numerous applications in different fields.

Seven

Relational Theory

"All of relational theory is built on Predicate calculus." - Chris Date.

In computer science and database management, the relational model is one of the fundamental concepts that underpin the design, development, and querying of relational databases. Two prominent branches of the relational model include relational algebra theory and relational calculus theory. Although we use both in the context of the relational model, they differ in terms of purpose, syntax, and application.

Overview of the relational model

Before we delve into the specifics of relational algebra and relational calculus, let us briefly discuss the relational model itself. To be truly clear, I am referring to the original relational model defined by Ted Codd in his papers on the relational model. When asking Google and other online resources about the definition of the relational model, the following is a general summary of what you will find:

"The relational model is a way to organize and manipulate information stored in databases. It represents data as relations, which are essentially tables with rows and columns. Each row in a relation represents a specific instance of an entity, while each column corresponds to a specific attribute of that entity. The relational model provides a foundation for data manipulation and querying using operations and rules that have been developed over the years."

This definition reminds me of the story of a person lost in a hot-air balloon. They see a person walking on the ground and yell at them, asking where they are. The response floats up: "You are in a balloon."

It is an accurate answer, but it could be more helpful.

We will elaborate on the concepts of relational algebra and relational calculus shortly, but before we do, let us understand the fundamental components of relational theory considering the previous sections on set theory, logic, and functions.

The following image is a table representing some data about the United States Declaration of Independence signers. It includes names, occupations, age, number of marriages, and the date of death and when they died.

As we describe these fundamental concepts, we will be referring to the following image:

Signers

Primary Key	Alternate Primary Key	Name	Last Name	First Name	State Rep	Age at Death
f8fd85f1-e57a-4a91-a727-bab9d9689a08	1	Adams, John	Adams	John	MA	90
39d4fc35-6a7d-4fb8-8a97-3c14a603d24d	2	Adams, Samuel	Adams	Samuel	MA	81
2459609b-839d-4b58-919b-1395c27c6acd	3	Bartlett, Josiah	Bartlett	Josiah	NH	65
1591c7a1-12a2-42f6-8248-c4d47be5f919	4	Braxton, Carter	Braxton	Carter	VA	61
6b04ef30-2b38-4a98-93dc-537d33eaec5f	5	Carroll, Charles of Carrollton	Carroll	Charles of Carrollton	MD	95
3507f42f-8a14-450c-80ef-64e37e1c26ba	6	Chase, Samuel	Chase	Samuel	MD	70
d51a21eb-4356-4f31-a33e-9c9ca2fe1c2e	7	Clark, Abraham	Clark	Abraham	NJ	68
50e0f3f4-2284-4f33-8564-9ce7d1ff96b6	8	Clymer, George	Clymer	George	PA	73
68d617c7-57fe-4363-86a4-3afdbe4aeef4	9	Ellery, William	Ellery	William	RI	92
47e8dc76-be88-41bc-8b95-d5f7c5e75692	10	Floyd, William	Floyd	William	NY	86
4280e444-a7a3-4936-ad85-e315a4770a8b	11	Franklin, Benjamin	Franklin	Benjamin	PA	84
d60da186-db1c-4f91-afb6-4fdf5b196f87	12	Gerry, Elbridge	Gerry	Elbridge	MA	70
218d3e01-c52a-4bb3-b435-ba184a541d9b	13	Gwinnett, Button	Gwinnett	Button	GA	42
13ad0e2a-ddd1-4d5f-92b0-2fb5611bcb07	14	Hall, Lyman	Hall	Lyman	GA	66
89e644b2-f8e0-4955-869f-908a02a845d3	15	Hancock, John	Hancock	John	MA	56

Primary Key	Alternate Primary Key	Name	Last Name	First Name	State Rep	Age at Death
1981166a-3551-4e4e-bf79-be93b6db660a	16	Harrison, Benjamin	Harrison	Benjamin	VA	65
814e4d37-bdc7-4b4b-b5d9-193c0f228770	17	Hart, John	Hart	John	NJ	68
7a156954-8ac8-452b-ab19-792c8f9201eb	18	Hewes, Joseph	Hewes	Joseph	NC	49
796d0c18-0753-47b9-ab43-b0e9695f4b99	19	Heyward Jr., Thomas	Heyward Jr.	Thomas	SC	62
c08ff135-f5af-43a5-b58e-e7cc179f052e	20	Hooper, William	Hooper	William	NC	48
ee7c71cd-86b7-4adc-a07b-327ed05a442e	21	Hopkins, Stephen	Hopkins	Stephen	RI	78
1ffef1fe-9887-49ff-945b-0f9b3536b7f5	22	Hopkinson, Francis	Hopkinson	Francis	NJ	53
8b3f5b3e-adb0-460b-8531-b0f7948b2fe6	23	Huntington, Samuel	Huntington	Samuel	CT	64
991ceb93-0956-48e1-96d4-d56dc61c6f15	24	Jefferson, Thomas	Jefferson	Thomas	VA	83
66b85cc9-ccc0-4142-b4ed-53f9ea82d7b2	25	Lee, Francis Lightfoot	Lee	Francis Lightfoot	VA	62
35575760-1056-43dc-8635-074fc624feb9	26	Lee, Richard Henry	Lee	Richard Henry	VA	62
ebde96a0-9b18-45ac-9a2c-7017d7114aeb	27	Lewis, Francis	Lewis	Francis	NY	89
883919e9-903d-4940-a21d-59f660779465	28	Livingston, Philip	Livingston	Philip	NY	62
f02510ec-19db-4a5e-a39c-d5fbdefaa8ab	29	Lynch Jr., Thomas	Lynch Jr.	Thomas	SC	30
b05126ba-e25c-40de-9a0e-fc7c9c727aa4	30	McKean, Thomas	McKean	Thomas	DE	83
80346877-228b-4327-a2f1-dfba75eb7738	31	Middleton, Arthur	Middleton	Arthur	SC	44

Primary Key	Alternate Primary Key	Name	Last Name	First Name	State Rep	Age at Death
6e95a235-f0d3-4e04-90b4-64acb0e1e52f	32	Morris, Lewis	Morris	Lewis	NY	71
e145c037-3193-4418-96f7-9f0d3390bae1	33	Morris, Robert	Morris	Robert	PA	72
5422469b-b7a6-46fb-9ac4-0561fa3db852	34	Morton, John	Morton	John	PA	53
7364d795-058c-4c3b-bbd9-76cabfaef5ca	35	Nelson Jr., Thomas	Nelson Jr.	Thomas	VA	50
b06fc560-fbf4-4928-997e-7f1103ee2220	36	Paca, William	Paca	William	MD	58
bd157b6d-3d15-4e8f-9ba7-9041c816ad95	37	Paine, Robert Treat	Paine	Robert Treat	MA	83
a2cc1ae3-9c6b-4af1-9223-50b8b1ab0f20	38	Penn, John	Penn	John	NC	48
dbaac539-9e4e-4042-9bd2-92db0520fc4b	39	Read, George	Read	George	DE	65
21f933aa-ed43-4086-aec6-02258c9ae068	40	Rodney, Caesar	Rodney	Caesar	DE	55
1e4a8dfd-e2ed-4170-9379-2f66bf321752	41	Ross, George	Ross	George	PA	49
3b1f5df9-9edf-4e65-8dd1-7ee994dea9ed	42	Rush, Benjamin Dr.	Rush	Benjamin Dr.	PA	67
148ec69b-2165-42ed-bdcb-e291efb8a9de	43	Rutledge, Edward	Rutledge	Edward	SC	50
01bb6786-bfc7-4458-8298-db7a96a612d5	44	Sherman, Roger	Sherman	Roger	CT	72
8bfc10d1-d94f-4ae5-8025-c5e52c245119	45	Smith, James	Smith	James	PA	87
daecc122-a990-4d26-87cd-46b32583e122	46	Stockton, Richard	Stockton	Richard	NJ	50
aca9d17e-3d7d-4c39-8024-c209e7b148b1	47	Stone, Thomas	Stone	Thomas	MD	44

Primary Key	Alternate Primary Key	Name	Last Name	First Name	State Rep	Age at Death
928de45f-fe0f-4181-aa41-973726d36d22	48	Taylor, George	Taylor	George	PA	65
adbf498d-0470-4e4a-b843-feeb84275373	49	Thornton, Matthew	Thornton	Matthew	NH	89
2f9fd03d-1d10-4339-ac95-ee8133f8427a	50	Walton, George	Walton	George	GA	63
b3848f86-0ea2-4118-9ec4-26ed41a36010	51	Whipple, William	Whipple	William	NH	55
635a9c5f-c2ad-4751-a27e-7e5a1d89f857	52	Williams, William	Williams	William	CT	80
766b9f25-ef38-4105-a399-cfc8a5d69f4d	53	Wilson, James	Wilson	James	PA	55
ac6abca3-8ac6-4284-8cb1-753dace6cc30	54	Witherspoon, John	Witherspoon	John	NJ	71
73f6546f-8492-42c1-aa43-398fd174aa69	55	Wolcott, Oliver	Wolcott	Oliver	CT	71
935145b6-a927-4120-b4e7-4e6ebafdcb8d	56	Wythe, George	Wythe	George	VA	80

A secondary table named Presidents would look like this:

Presidents

Position	Name	Party	Term Start	State of Birth	Born	Died
1	Washington	Federalist	1/20/1789	Virginia	2/22/1732	12/14/1799
2	J. Adams	Federalist	1/20/1797	Massachusetts	10/30/1735	7/4/1826
3	Jefferson	Democratic-Republican	1/20/1801	Virginia	4/13/1743	7/4/1826
4	Madison	Democratic-Republican	1/20/1809	Virginia	3/16/1751	6/28/1836
5	Monroe	Democratic-Republican	1/20/1817	Virginia	4/28/1758	7/4/1831
6	J. Q. Adams	Democratic-Republican	1/20/1825	Massachusetts	7/11/1767	2/23/1848
7	Jackson	Democratic	1/20/1829	South Carolina	3/15/1767	6/8/1845
8	Van Buren	Democratic	1/20/1837	New York	12/5/1782	7/24/1862
9	W. H. Harrison	Whig	1/20/1841	Virginia	2/9/1773	4/4/1841

Position	Name	Party	Term Start	State of Birth	Born	Died
10	Tyler	Whig	1/20/1841	Virginia	3/29/1790	1/18/1862
11	Polk	Democratic	1/20/1845	North Carolina	11/2/1795	6/15/1849
12	Taylor	Whig	1/20/1849	Virginia	11/24/1784	7/9/1850
13	Fillmore	Whig	1/20/1850	New York	1/7/1800	3/8/1874
14	Pierce	Democratic	1/20/1853	New Hampshire	11/23/1804	10/8/1869
15	Buchanan	Democratic	1/20/1857	Pennsylvania	4/23/1791	6/1/1868
16	Lincoln	Republican	1/20/1861	Kentucky	2/12/1809	4/15/1865
17	A. Johnson	Union	1/20/1865	North Carolina	12/29/1808	7/31/1875
18	Grant	Republican	1/20/1869	Ohio	4/27/1822	7/23/1885
19	Hayes	Republican	1/20/1877	Ohio	10/4/1822	1/17/1893
20	Garfield	Republican	1/20/1881	Ohio	11/19/1831	9/19/1881
21	Arthur	Republican	1/20/1881	Vermont	10/5/1829	11/18/1886
22	Cleveland	Democratic	1/20/1885	New Jersey	3/18/1837	6/24/1908
23	B. Harrison	Republican	1/20/1889	Ohio	8/20/1833	3/13/1901
24	Cleveland	Democratic	1/20/1893	New Jersey	3/18/1837	6/24/1908
25	McKinley	Republican	1/20/1897	Ohio	1/29/1843	9/14/1901
26	T. Roosevelt	Republican	1/20/1901	New York	10/27/1858	1/6/1919
27	Taft	Republican	1/20/1909	Ohio	9/15/1857	3/8/1930
28	Wilson	Democratic	1/20/1913	Virginia	12/28/1856	2/3/1924
29	Harding	Republican	1/20/1921	Ohio	11/2/1865	8/2/1923
30	Coolidge	Republican	1/20/1923	Vermont	7/4/1872	1/5/1933
31	Hoover	Republican	1/20/1929	Iowa	8/10/1874	10/20/1964
32	F. D. Roosevelt	Democratic	1/20/1933	New York	1/30/1882	4/12/1945
33	Truman	Democratic	1/20/1945	Missouri	5/8/1884	12/26/1972
34	Eisenhower	Republican	1/20/1953	Texas	10/14/1890	3/28/1969
35	Kennedy	Democratic	1/20/1961	Massachusetts	5/29/1917	11/22/1963
36	L. B. Johnson	Democratic	1/20/1963	Texas	8/27/1908	1/22/1973
37	Nixon	Republican	1/20/1969	California	1/9/1913	4/22/1994
38	Ford	Republican	1/20/1974	Nebraska	7/14/1913	12/26/2006
39	Carter	Democratic	1/20/1977	Georgia	10/1/1924	
40	Reagan	Republican	1/20/1981	Illinois	2/6/1911	6/5/2004
41	G.H.W. Bush	Republican	1/20/1989	Massachusetts	6/12/1924	
42	Clinton	Democratic	1/20/1993	Arkansas	8/19/1946	
43	G. W. Bush	Republican	1/20/2001	Connecticut	7/6/1946	
44	Obama	Democratic	1/20/2009	Hawaii	8/4/1961	

What we today think of as a column in this two-dimensional representation of a table is a set together with a domain definition. Referring to the above illustration, the first column is defined as the set with the domain "primary key." Today, we tend to think of this as an attribute that has a name and a data type. In most databases, the data type will affect the amount of storage to be used by the column in the table (more on this later).

> *The term relational comes from the relationship between these attributes in the definition of this structure.*

The "relation" is the definition of the structure. There is another term used by both Codd and Date called a "RelVar".[17] A RelVar is an instantiation of the definition of the relation. A RelVar would be what we consider today to be a row in the table. The RelVar is a finitary relation[18] between the sets that are defined as attributes.

Each column or attribute is a set, and the structural definition of a relation is a set of attributes related to each other. The instantiation of which is a tuple[19] , and since the definition of an instantiation of a relation is a RelVar this means that the tuple of that data is defined as a RelVar, that is unique according to the definition of the relation. Quoting from the footnote on the Finitary Relation: "In

---

[17] https://en.wikipedia.org/wiki/Relvar

[18] https://en.wikipedia.org/wiki/Finitary_relation

[19] https://en.wikipedia.org/wiki/Tuple

mathematics, a finitary relation over sets X1, ..., Xn is a subset of the Cartesian product X1 × ⋯ × Xn; that is, it is a set of n-tuples (x1, ..., xn) consisting of elements xi in Xi."

The following is the set representation of the first few rows of the data shown in the image above:

{

{335d53ae-a701-41d7-9fb8-8ad5b2a75e3b,1,"Adams, John", Adams, John, MA,10/30/1735,"Quincy,MA",40,Lawyer,1,5,7/4/1826,90 },

{23c194b3-d1e1-448f-9c37-b9f993fb440a,2,"Adams, Samuel", Adams, Samuel, MA,9/27/1722, "Boston, MA", 53, Merchant,2,2,10/2/1803, 81},

{07846bfa-a73e-4d8e-aec4-6d280ee9e43c,3,"Bartlett, Josiah", Bartlett, Josiah, NH,11/21/1729, "Amesbury, MA",46,Physician,1,12,5/19/1795,65}

}

From the perspective of predicate logic, the first RelVar states:

Signer "335d53ae-a701-41d7-9fb8-8ad5b2a75e3b" has an alternate key of 1, and a Name of "Adams, John", whose Last Name is "Adams", and First Name is "John" was the State Rep from "MA", his Birth date is "10/30/1735", Birthplace was "Quincy, MA", had the Age in 1776 of 40, whose Occupation was Lawyer, and number of Marriages was 1, the Number of Children was 5, Date of Death "7/4/1826", and whose Age at Death was 90.

One way to interpret this is as a sentence whose noun is the primary key, and the other attributes are adjectives or various parts of speech. My high school teacher making me diagram sentences would be laughing, but that comes a little later.

The design of a table is much like the design of a sentence.

It was only one of the ways those sentence diagrams would haunt me throughout my adult life. Incidentally, by looking at this relation definition, you will see that there is no room for the actual values to be NULL. Chris Date has a pet peeve about this, and he will educate you for some time on why introducing NULL into the SQL standard was an incredible mistake. This is the proper way to interpret the definition of a relation. All these predicates are dependent on the primary key. The order is irrelevant for relational theory. However, this ability to turn the definition of a table into a proper sentence is something unique to relational theory.

Relational algebra theory

Relational algebra theory is a procedural query language for relational databases. It provides a set of operations to perform queries on relations, enabling data retrieval and manipulation. These operations are based on set theory and logic and are used to express queries in a concise and declarative manner. Relational algebra operations include selection, projection, Cartesian product, union, intersection, difference, and others. These operations can be combined and nested to form complex queries. Let us dive into each operation and explain it with an example:

- **Selection (σ):** The selection operation allows us to retrieve a subset of rows from a relation that satisfies a given condition. For instance, consider a relation called "Signers" with attributes "Name" and "Age at Death". You can use selection to find the signers of the Declaration of Independence who are above the age of 50: σ("Age at Death" > 50) (Signers).

- **Projection (π):** The projection operation enables us to retrieve a subset of columns from a relation. It helps us extract only the attributes in which we are interested. For example, if we have a relation "Presidents" with various attributes including "Name" and "State of Birth", we can use projection to retrieve only those two attributes: π(Name, "State of Birth")(Presidents).

- **Cartesian Product (×):** The Cartesian product operation combines rows from two relations to create a new relation. We denote it by the "×" symbol. For instance, if we have two relations, "Signers" with attributes "Name" and "Age at Death", and "Presidents" with attributes "Name" and "Party", using the Cartesian product will result in a new relation containing all combinations: Signers × Presidents.

- **Union (∪):** The union operation combines two relations, keeping only distinct rows. The"∪"

symbol denotes it. For example, if we have two relations, "Signers1" and "Signers2", both with attributes "Name" and "Age at Death", the union operation will give us a relation with distinct records: Signers1 ∪ Signers2.

- **Intersection (∩):** The intersection operation combines two relations by retaining only the common rows between them. The"∩"symbol denotes it. For instance, if we have two relations, "Signers1" and "Signers2", both with attributes "Name" and "Age," the intersection operation will give us a relation with records existing in both relations: Students1 ∩ Students2.

- **Difference (-):** The difference operation compares two relations and returns only the rows that exist in the first relation but not in the second relation. The "-" symbol denotes it. For example, if we have two relations, "Signers1" and "Signers2," both with attributes "Name" and "Age," the difference operation will return a relation with records from "Signers1" that are not present in "Signers2": Signers1 - Signers2.

Relational calculus theory

Relational calculus theory, on the other hand, is a declarative query language that focuses on describing *what data to retrieve* from a relation rather than *how to retrieve it*. Relational calculus specifies the characteristics and properties of desired results without specifying the actual process or steps to obtain those results. It enables users to express queries in the form of logical formulas or statements.

There are two types of relational calculus: Tuple Relational Calculus (TRC) and Domain Relational Calculus (DRC). Let us explore each of them with examples:

- **Tuple Relational Calculus (TRC):** TRC operates on the individual tuples of a relation and uses variables, quantifiers, and logical formulas to express queries. It allows the user to select tuples that satisfy a specified condition. Consider the relation "Signers" with attributes "Name" and "Age at Death" once again. To find students above the age of 50 using TRC, we can formulate the query as follows: { s | ∃ s ∈ Signers (s."Age at Death" > 50) }. Here, "s" is a variable, "∃" denotes the existential quantifier, "s.Age at Death > 20" is the condition, and "Signers" is the relation. This query reads as "Retrieve the tuple 's' from the relation 'Signers' for which it exists such that the Age at Death of 's' is greater than 50."

- **Domain Relational Calculus (DRC):** As the name suggests, DRC operates on the attributes or domains of a relation. It uses variables, quantifiers, and formulas to express queries. DRC is like TRC but focuses on describing the desired properties of attribute values. Let us continue with the "Signers" relation. If we want to retrieve the names of the signers above the age of 50 using DRC, the query can be expressed as {s.Name | ∃ s ∈ Signers (s.Age at Death > 50) }. Here, "s.Name" represents the attribute we want to retrieve, and the rest of the query is like the TRC example. This query can be read as "Retrieve the names of Signers 's' from the relation 'Signers' for which it exists such that the age at death of 's' is greater than 50."

Difference between relational algebra and relational calculus

Now that we have explored the basic concepts and examples of relational algebra and relational calculus, let us summarize their key differences:

- **Purpose:** Relational algebra focuses on the procedural aspects of querying and manipulating relational databases, while relational calculus focuses on the declarative aspects of expressing queries more logically and descriptively.

- **Syntax:** Relational algebra has a well-defined set of operations, such as selection, projection, and set operations, which manipulate relations through set and logic-based operations. Relational calculus, on the other hand, relies on logical formulas, variables, and quantifiers to describe the characteristics of desired results.

- **Usage:** Relational algebra is closer to actual implementation and is often used as the basis for query languages like SQL. It provides a framework for constructing complex queries by combining and nesting operations. Relational calculus, however, is more abstract and is used for formal reasoning, query optimization, and database theory.

- **Compactness:** Relational algebra is typically more concise and compact in terms of representing queries, as it relies on a predefined set of operations and syntax. In contrast, relational calculus is often more verbose, as it involves logical formulas and quantifiers to describe the desired results fully.

Relational algebra theory and relational calculus theory are two distinct but interconnected branches of the relational model. While Relational algebra focuses on procedural operations used to manipulate relations, relational calculus relies on logical formulas and quantifiers to specify desired results.

Understanding the difference between these two theories is crucial for effectively designing, querying, and managing relational databases. Whether you work with relational algebraic expressions or declarative calculus formulas, both theories contribute to the foundation of modern relational database systems.

EIGHT

SQL

"SQL: the language of love in the data world – we join tables, select the best matches, and find our perfect records." - Anon

Now, on to Structured Query Language (SQL), which is more relational calculus than relational algebra. SQL was not my first data manipulation language. That would have been dBase, as mentioned earlier. After that, I learned a language called Natural, which is strongly associated with the ADABAS database management system.

I had to learn SQL on my own in preparation for a world where Natural and ADABAS were not the predominant database tools. I learned Oracle SQL first, followed by T-SQL for SQL Server. Eventually, I learned the dialect for MySQL, PostgreSQL, ClickHouse, and RedShift, and currently, I now work almost exclusively with Snowflake. The Snowflake documentation is the clearest when explaining syntax and object management concepts. While all database technologies have documentation explaining their take on the standards and how things are implemented, I will refer to Snowflake documentation to have a consistent external set of references.

Every Relational Database Management System (RDBMS) has implemented SQL to define and manipulate data and objects within its databases. SQL standards exist according to ANSI and ISO. However, each vendor tends to enrich their implementation so that SQL that works on one database does not work on another. Historically, in 2003, support was added to the SQL standard for XML, and in 2016, support was added for JSON.

While these (XML and JSON) are not explicitly part of relational theory, they can be manipulated with functions in SQL. We will talk about this concept of functions and the manipulation of sets of data more when we cover the specific data manipulation language subset of SQL.

Structured Query Language (SQL) is a domain-specific language designed and implemented to define data structures and database objects (DDL), to manipulate data within tables and views (DML), to allow or prevent access to database objects (DCL), or to create transactions around a set of DML statements (TCL).

TABLE

SQL works exclusively with tables. In an RDBMS, a relational table is defined as a collection of related data organized into rows and columns. The structure of a table is based on the principles of relational theory discussed previously, which defines a relation as a set of tuples (rows) with the same attributes (columns). Each tuple in a relation represents a unique combination of values across all columns.

RDBMS supports various data types for attributes, including numeric, string, date, time, and Boolean. Each attribute must be assigned a specific data type when defining a table to ensure data consistency and accuracy.

Additionally, each table should have a primary key, which is a column or set of columns that uniquely identifies each row in the table. The primary key constraint ensures that each row in the table is unique and provides a way to efficiently access and update specific rows.

A foreign key is a column or set of columns in one table that refers to the primary key of another table. This establishes a relationship between the two tables, where the foreign key represents a reference to a specific row in the other table. Foreign keys enforce referential integrity, ensuring that the data in one table is consistent with the data in another.

The table in a relational database is what is thought of when talking about "structured data."

Signers

Primary Key	Alternate Primary Key	Name	Last Name	First Name	State Rep	Age at Death
f8fd85f1-e57a-4a91-a727-bab9d9689a08	1	Adams, John	Adams	John	MA	90
39d4fc35-6a7d-4fb8-8a97-3c14a603d24d	2	Adams, Samuel	Adams	Samuel	MA	81
2459609b-839d-4b58-919b-1395c27c6acd	3	Bartlett, Josiah	Bartlett	Josiah	NH	65
1591c7a1-12a2-42f6-8248-c4d47be5f919	4	Braxton, Carter	Braxton	Carter	VA	61
6b04ef30-2b38-4a98-93dc-537d33eaec5f	5	Carroll, Charles of Carrollton	Carroll	Charles of Carrollton	MD	95
3507f42f-8a14-450c-80ef-64e37e1c26ba	6	Chase, Samuel	Chase	Samuel	MD	70
d51a21eb-4356-4f31-a33e-9c9ca2fe1c2e	7	Clark, Abraham	Clark	Abraham	NJ	68
50e0f3f4-2284-4f33-8564-9ce7d1ff96b6	8	Clymer, George	Clymer	George	PA	73
68d617c7-57fe-4363-86a4-3afdbe4aeef4	9	Ellery, William	Ellery	William	RI	92
47e8dc76-be88-41bc-8b95-d5f7c5e75692	10	Floyd, William	Floyd	William	NY	86
4280e444-a7a3-4936-ad85-e315a4770a8b	11	Franklin, Benjamin	Franklin	Benjamin	PA	84
d60da186-db1c-4f91-afb6-4fdf5b196f87	12	Gerry, Elbridge	Gerry	Elbridge	MA	70
218d3e01-c52a-4bb3-b435-ba184a541d9b	13	Gwinnett, Button	Gwinnett	Button	GA	42
13ad0e2a-ddd1-4d5f-92b0-2fb5611bcb07	14	Hall, Lyman	Hall	Lyman	GA	66
89e644b2-f8e0-4955-869f-908a02a845d3	15	Hancock, John	Hancock	John	MA	56

Primary Key	Alternate Primary Key	Name	Last Name	First Name	State Rep	Age at Death
1981166a-3551-4e4e-bf79-be93b6db660a	16	Harrison, Benjamin	Harrison	Benjamin	VA	65
814e4d37-bdc7-4b4b-b5d9-193c0f228770	17	Hart, John	Hart	John	NJ	68
7a156954-8ac8-452b-ab19-792c8f9201eb	18	Hewes, Joseph	Hewes	Joseph	NC	49
796d0c18-0753-47b9-ab43-b0e9695f4b99	19	Heyward Jr., Thomas	Heyward Jr.	Thomas	SC	62
c08ff135-f5af-43a5-b58e-e7cc179f052e	20	Hooper, William	Hooper	William	NC	48
ee7c71cd-86b7-4adc-a07b-327ed05a442e	21	Hopkins, Stephen	Hopkins	Stephen	RI	78
1ffef1fe-9887-49ff-945b-0f9b3536b7f5	22	Hopkinson, Francis	Hopkinson	Francis	NJ	53
8b3f5b3e-adb0-460b-8531-b0f7948b2fe6	23	Huntington, Samuel	Huntington	Samuel	CT	64
991ceb93-0956-48e1-96d4-d56dc61c6f15	24	Jefferson, Thomas	Jefferson	Thomas	VA	83
66b85cc9-ccc0-4142-b4ed-53f9ea82d7b2	25	Lee, Francis Lightfoot	Lee	Francis Lightfoot	VA	62
35575760-1056-43dc-8635-074fc624feb9	26	Lee, Richard Henry	Lee	Richard Henry	VA	62
ebde96a0-9b18-45ac-9a2c-7017d7114aeb	27	Lewis, Francis	Lewis	Francis	NY	89
883919e9-903d-4940-a21d-59f660779465	28	Livingston, Philip	Livingston	Philip	NY	62
f02510ec-19db-4a5e-a39c-d5fbdefaa8ab	29	Lynch Jr., Thomas	Lynch Jr.	Thomas	SC	30
b05126ba-e25c-40de-9a0e-fc7c9c727aa4	30	McKean, Thomas	McKean	Thomas	DE	83
80346877-228b-4327-a2f1-dfba75eb7738	31	Middleton, Arthur	Middleton	Arthur	SC	44

Primary Key	Alternate Primary Key	Name	Last Name	First Name	State Rep	Age at Death
6e95a235-f0d3-4e04-90b4-64acb0e1e52f	32	Morris, Lewis	Morris	Lewis	NY	71
e145c037-3193-4418-96f7-9f0d3390bae1	33	Morris, Robert	Morris	Robert	PA	72
5422469b-b7a6-46fb-9ac4-0561fa3db852	34	Morton, John	Morton	John	PA	53
7364d795-058c-4c3b-bbd9-76cabfaef5ca	35	Nelson Jr., Thomas	Nelson Jr.	Thomas	VA	50
b06fc560-fbf4-4928-997e-7f1103ee2220	36	Paca, William	Paca	William	MD	58
bd157b6d-3d15-4e8f-9ba7-9041c816ad95	37	Paine, Robert Treat	Paine	Robert Treat	MA	83
a2cc1ae3-9c6b-4af1-9223-50b8b1ab0f20	38	Penn, John	Penn	John	NC	48
dbaac539-9e4e-4042-9bd2-92db0520fc4b	39	Read, George	Read	George	DE	65
21f933aa-ed43-4086-aec6-02258c9ae068	40	Rodney, Caesar	Rodney	Caesar	DE	55
1e4a8dfd-e2ed-4170-9379-2f66bf321752	41	Ross, George	Ross	George	PA	49
3b1f5df9-9edf-4e65-8dd1-7ee994dea9ed	42	Rush, Benjamin Dr.	Rush	Benjamin Dr.	PA	67
148ec69b-2165-42ed-bdcb-e291efb8a9de	43	Rutledge, Edward	Rutledge	Edward	SC	50
01bb6786-bfc7-4458-8298-db7a96a612d5	44	Sherman, Roger	Sherman	Roger	CT	72
8bfc10d1-d94f-4ae5-8025-c5e52c245119	45	Smith, James	Smith	James	PA	87
daecc122-a990-4d26-87cd-46b32583e122	46	Stockton, Richard	Stockton	Richard	NJ	50
aca9d17e-3d7d-4c39-8024-c209e7b148b1	47	Stone, Thomas	Stone	Thomas	MD	44

Primary Key	Alternate Primary Key	Name	Last Name	First Name	State Rep	Age at Death
928de45f-fe0f-4181-aa41-973726d36d22	48	Taylor, George	Taylor	George	PA	65
adbf498d-0470-4e4a-b843-feeb84275373	49	Thornton, Matthew	Thornton	Matthew	NH	89
2f9fd03d-1d10-4339-ac95-ee8133f8427a	50	Walton, George	Walton	George	GA	63
b3848f86-0ea2-4118-9ec4-26ed41a36010	51	Whipple, William	Whipple	William	NH	55
635a9c5f-c2ad-4751-a27e-7e5a1d89f857	52	Williams, William	Williams	William	CT	80
766b9f25-ef38-4105-a399-cfc8a5d69f4d	53	Wilson, James	Wilson	James	PA	55
ac6abca3-8ac6-4284-8cb1-753dace6cc30	54	Witherspoon, John	Witherspoon	John	NJ	71
73f6546f-8492-42c1-aa43-398fd174aa69	55	Wolcott, Oliver	Wolcott	Oliver	CT	71
935145b6-a927-4120-b4e7-4e6ebafdcb8d	56	Wythe, George	Wythe	George	VA	80

A relational database is a database that manages what was initially called relations but is implemented as tables. The term relation refers to the structure of a table. The key of a table is supposed to be unique; in the example above, it could be a Universally Unique Identifier (UUID), and an alternative is simply an integer starting from one. Each of the columns defined in the table is "related" to the primary key.

The design of a table will become important later when we talk about joining data together, including joining the semi-structured data to the structured tables in our database.

In the table sense, a key is a unique column. In many databases, we index these keys for performance. Some databases including Snowflake may have an alternate approach to enforcing uniqueness. Specifically, Snowflake has the concept of a Clustering Key.[20]

A clustering key is a mechanism that Snowflake uses internally to organize the partitions on which the data is physically stored. Delving into the details of Snowflake's physical architecture is beyond the scope of this book. However, it is important to mention that the performance of retrieving data from the Data Structures can be influenced by either the proper use or improper use of a clustering key.

Setting a clustering key on a table should not be done arbitrarily. Take some time to understand how the data comes into a table, what the data type is, how frequently data is added, and if there are any null values. These are all things to consider when deciding on a clustering key.

DDL

The Data Definition Language (DDL) is the subset of SQL that creates and manages various database objects.

---

[20] https://docs.snowflake.com/en/user-guide/tables-clustering-keys

Snowflake has extensive documentation about the objects that can be managed.[21] Here is a brief overview:

CREATE

Create is the command to create an object. We use it to establish the initial structure of an Enrichment Platform, starting with creating a new database. The syntax for CREATE DATABASE is as follows:

```
CREATE DATABASE <database name>
```

In addition to databases, we can also use the CREATE command to create tables, views, schemas, stored procedures, and other objects the data engineer requires. Each object type has its own unique set of options to specify in the CREATE statement.

When creating a database object, it is essential to consider the following factors:

- **Object type:** The type of object you are creating will determine the syntax of the CREATE statement and the available options.

- **Object name:** The name of the object must be unique within the database or schema in which it is created.

---

[21] https://docs.snowflake.com/en/sql-eference/sql/create.html

- **Data types:** The data types of the columns in a table must be specified in the CREATE statement.

- **Constraints:** Constraints can be used to enforce data integrity and ensure that the data in a table is valid.

- **Indexes:** Indexes can improve query performance by providing a faster way to access data.

The CREATE command is a powerful tool for creating various objects within a Snowflake database. By understanding the syntax and options available for each object type, data engineers can create optimized objects for performance and security.

We can also combine the CREATE statement with the SELECT statement to create a new table based on the results of a query. This is known as a "create table ... as select" (CTAS) statement. The syntax for a CTAS statement is as follows:

```
CREATE TABLE <table name> AS SELECT <columns> FROM <table name>
```

CTAS statements are a convenient way to create new tables that are derived from existing data. They can also be used to create tables with a specific structure or to perform data transformations.

ALTER

Alter is the command to modify an object in case its use has changed or if a typo was issued when creating it. It is commonly used to change tables, views, indexes, stored procedures, and other database elements.

One of the primary uses of the ALTER command is to modify the structure of a table. This includes adding or removing columns, changing the data type of a column, modifying column constraints, or renaming columns. For example, if a user realizes that a column is missing or needs to be renamed, the ALTER command can be used to make the necessary changes without having to recreate the entire table.

Another everyday use of the ALTER command is to modify a table's properties. This includes changing the table's storage options, such as setting it to use a specific type of index or specifying the initial size of the table's data file. Additionally, the ALTER command can be used to modify the table's access permissions, such as granting or revoking access to specific users or groups.

The ALTER command can also modify the structure and properties of views, indexes, stored procedures, and other database objects. For example, we can use it to add or remove columns from a view, modify the definition of an index, or change the parameters of a stored procedure.

When using the ALTER command, it is essential to exercise caution and understand the potential impact of the changes being made. Specific ALTER operations, such as removing columns or modifying primary key constraints, can significantly impact the database's integrity and performance. Test any ALTER operations in a development or staging environment before implementing them in a production environment.

Here are some additional examples of how the ALTER command can be used for:

Adding a new column to a table:

```
ALTER TABLE customers ADD COLUMN email VARCHAR(255);
```

Changing the data type of a column:

```
ALTER TABLE customers ALTER COLUMN age INT;
```

Modifying a column constraint:

```
ALTER TABLE customers ALTER COLUMN name SET NOT NULL;
```

Renaming a column:

```
ALTER TABLE customers RENAME COLUMN name TO customer_name;
```

Changing the storage options of a table:

```
ALTER TABLE customers SET STORAGE (TYPE=HEAP);
```

Granting access to a table:

```
ALTER TABLE customers GRANT SELECT, INSERT, UPDATE, DELETE TO
user_group;
```

Revoking access to a table:

```
ALTER TABLE customers REVOKE SELECT, INSERT, UPDATE, DELETE
FROM user_group;
```

DROP

The DROP command completely removes an object. The Drop command is a destructive command that cannot be undone, so use it with caution. The DROP command can be used to delete tables, views, indexes, constraints, and other database objects.

The syntax of the DROP command is as follows:

DROP [OBJECT TYPE] [OBJECT NAME];

Where:

OBJECT TYPE is the type of object to be deleted.

OBJECT NAME is the name of the object to be deleted.

For example, to delete a table named customers, you would use the following command:

```
DROP TABLE customers;
```

Use the DROP command to delete multiple objects at once. For example, to delete the table customers and the table orders, you would use the following command:

```
DROP TABLE customers, orders;
```

It is important to note that we cannot use the DROP command to delete objects referenced by other objects. For example, if the orders table references the customers table, you cannot delete the customers table without first deleting the orders table.

If you are unsure whether other objects reference an object, you can use a command to check. The GET_OBJECT_REFERENCES command will list all the objects that reference a given object.

TRUNCATE

Truncate is the command to mark the table as empty but retain its structure and the permissions assigned to it. Unlike the DELETE statement, which allows for selective deletion of rows based on specified criteria, TRUNCATE removes all rows without any exceptions.

Use the TRUNCATE command to remove a large volume of data quickly and efficiently from a table. It is also useful when resetting a table to its initial state, as it removes all rows and resets the auto-increment column values to their starting points.

One key benefit of using TRUNCATE is its speed. Compared to DELETE, which needs to evaluate each row and apply the deletion criteria, TRUNCATE performs a much faster operation by allocating the storage space occupied by the table's data.

However, it is essential to note that TRUNCATE is an irreversible operation, meaning we cannot recover the deleted data. Therefore, it is crucial to carefully consider the implications before executing a TRUNCATE command, especially on tables containing valuable or sensitive data.

Here are some additional points to consider regarding the TRUNCATE command:

TRUNCATE does not fire database triggers or execute cascading deletes on related tables.

It does not log any redo information, making it a non-transactional operation.

TRUNCATE acquires an exclusive lock on the table, preventing other concurrent operations until the command completes.

We can use the TRUNCATE command for maintenance tasks or when dealing with temporary or staging tables.

It is not recommended for use on large tables in production environments due to its irreversible nature and potential impact on performance.

TRUNCATE is a powerful command that can quickly and efficiently remove all rows from a table. However, it is vital to understand its implications and use it cautiously to avoid unintended data loss.

COMMENT

We can add comments to all objects within Snowflake. It is an excellent practice to put comments specifically on table structures. Comments that describe what a table or column is to be used for as part of the design are an example of metadata. We will come back to the topic of metadata.

They allow you to add additional information and context to your tables, columns, and other objects, making it easier for others to understand their purpose and usage.

Here are some of the benefits of using comments:

- **Improved readability**: Comments can make your code more readable and understandable, especially for those unfamiliar with the specific objects or their purpose.

- **Documentation**: Comments can serve as documentation for your objects, providing information about their design, usage, and any specific requirements or limitations.

- Collaboration: Comments can facilitate collaboration by allowing multiple users to contribute to the understanding and maintaining of the objects.

RELATIONAL THEORY • 117

- **Metadata**: Comments can be a valuable source of metadata, providing information about the objects that can be used for various purposes, such as data lineage and impact analysis.

Including comments on all your database objects is good practice, but they are crucial for table structures. Table comments can provide information about the purpose of the table, its relationship to other tables, and any specific usage considerations. Column comments can give information about the meaning and usage of each column, including its data type, constraints, and any default values.

We can add comments to objects using the COMMENT ON statement. For example, the following statement adds a comment to the "Customers" table:

```
COMMENT ON TABLE Customers IS 'This table stores customer
information.';
```

Comments can also be added to columns using the COMMENT ON COLUMN statement. For example, the following statement adds a comment to the "Email" column of the "Customers" table:

```
COMMENT ON COLUMN Customers.Email IS 'The email address of the
customer.';
```

Comments are an essential part of any well-designed Snowflake database. Adding comments to your objects can improve their readability, documentation, collaboration, and metadata.

CLONE

Clone is a command specific to Snowflake, and I encourage you to read the Snowflake documentation about this command.[22] It is beneficial for creating non-production environments, such as development, testing, and staging environments.

One key benefit of using CLONE is that it creates a semantic copy of the source database. This means the data is logically separated from the source database but still physically resides in the same storage. This allows for independent operations on the cloned database without affecting the source database.

For example, you can run queries, update data, and create new objects in the cloned database without impacting the source database. This makes it an ideal environment for testing changes, developing new features, or running performance tests.

Another advantage of CLONE is that it is a quick and efficient process. Snowflake uses a copy-on-write mechanism, meaning it only creates new physical storage when data is modified in the cloned database. This

---

[22] https://docs.snowflake.com/en/user-guide/object-clone.html

minimizes the amount of time and resources required to make the clone.

Here are some specific use cases for the CLONE command:

- **Development and testing:** Create a cloned database for development and testing purposes. This will allow developers to work on new features and bug fixes without affecting the production database.

- **Staging:** Create a cloned database as a staging environment for deploying new features or updates before they are released to production.

- **Reporting and analytics:** Create a cloned database for reporting and analytics purposes. This will allow business analysts to run queries without impacting the performance of the production database.

- **Disaster recovery:** Create a cloned database as a disaster recovery measure, ensuring that you have a backup of your data in case of a hardware failure or natural disaster.

It is important to note that the CLONE command has some limitations. For example, you cannot clone a database currently being used for a restore operation. Additionally, database objects, such as materialized views and external tables, are not cloned by default.

Overall, the CLONE command is a valuable tool for managing non-production environments in Snowflake. It provides a quick and efficient way to create copies of existing databases, allowing for independent operations and testing without affecting the source database.

DML

The Data Manipulation Language (DML) is the portion of SQL that manipulates data within the defined tables. These statements are generally referred to as part of the Create, Read, Update, Delete (CRUD) operations for the data itself rather than the database objects.

SELECT

The SELECT statement is the most used in all of SQL. Numerous examples online and in books talk extensively about this statement. Just as so many others have written about this statement, we will cover many options of the SELECT statement below. It allows users to specify which columns and rows to include in the resulting dataset, making it a powerful tool for data querying and analysis. One of the critical things to remember about the SELECT statement is that it always returns a table-like structure consisting of rows and columns, which can be further processed or manipulated using other SQL statements.

The SELECT statement and its various clauses provide a powerful mechanism for data retrieval, aggregation, sorting, and filtering. By combining these elements, users can extract meaningful information from their databases, gain insights, and make informed decisions based on the data.

All the CRUD operations can use the WHERE clause depending on the nature of the original command.

INSERT

The insert statement will insert data into a table that has already been defined. Like the CTAS statement mentioned before, an Insert can also be done from a SELECT statement: "INSERT into ... SELECT ..." For applications that are collecting data to provide to the Enrichment platform, the Insert, Update, and Delete commands will be "wrapped in a transaction."[23] This allows users to populate the table with specific values across its columns.

The syntax for the INSERT statement consists of the following components:

- **INSERT INTO:** This keyword combination initiates the INSERT statement and specifies the target table where we insert the new data.

- Column names: After the table name, you can optionally list the names of the columns in which you want to insert data. If you omit this, values will be inserted into all columns of the table.

---

[23] https://docs.snowflake.com/en/sql-reference/transactions.html

- **VALUES**: This keyword introduces the list of values to insert into the specified columns.

- **SELECT**: Instead of providing explicit values, you can also use a SELECT statement within the INSERT statement. This allows you to insert data from another table or the result set of a query.

For applications collecting data to provide to an Enrichment platform, the INSERT, UPDATE, and DELETE commands are often "wrapped in a transaction." A transaction is a set of database operations that are executed as a single unit. If any of the operations within the transaction fail, we roll the entire transaction back, ensuring data integrity and consistency.

Wrapping the data manipulation commands in a transaction provides several benefits:

- **Atomicity**: A transaction ensures that either all the operations within it succeed or none of them do. This prevents partial updates or insertions, maintaining data integrity.

- **Isolation**: Transactions isolate the changes made by one user or process from other concurrent transactions, ensuring that multiple users do not inconsistently modify data simultaneously.

- **Durability**: Once a transaction is committed, the changes made to the database become permanent, even in the event of a system failure.

By using transactions, applications can ensure that the data they insert, update, or delete is handled reliably and consistently, minimizing the risk of data corruption or inconsistencies in the Enrichment platform.

UPDATE

The Update STATEMENT modifies data that already exists in an existing table. It does not work within a JSON or XML structure but only for a table. The update statement allows you to change specific columns or rows without having to rewrite the entire table, making it a very efficient way to update large datasets.

The UPDATE statement has the following basic syntax:

```
UPDATE table_name
SET column_name = new_value
WHERE condition;
```

The table_name specifies the table that you want to update. The column_name specifies the column or columns that you want to update. The new_value is the new value that you want to assign to the specified column(s). The WHERE clause specifies the condition to meet to perform the update. For example, the following statement updates the "price" column of the "products" table, setting it to "100" for all products with an "id" greater than 10:

```
UPDATE products
SET price = 100
WHERE id > 10;
```

You can also use the UPDATE statement to update multiple columns at once. For example, the following statement updates both the "price" and "quantity" columns of the "products" table:

```
UPDATE products
SET price = 100, quantity = 20
WHERE id > 10;
```

We can use the UPDATE statement to perform a variety of data modifications, including:

- Changing the value of a single column
- Changing the values of multiple columns
- Setting a column to a specific value
- Adding a value to a column
- Subtracting a value from a column
- Multiplying a column by a value
- Dividing a column by a value

The UPDATE statement is a powerful tool for quickly and easily updating data in a table. However, it is essential to exercise caution when using it, as it can potentially delete or modify data if it is not used correctly.

DELETE

The DELETE statement is a powerful SQL tool that removes specific rows or sets of rows from a database table. It allows users to delete unwanted or outdated data from a table, maintaining the integrity and accuracy of the database.

The syntax of the DELETE statement is as follows:

```
DELETE FROM table_name
WHERE condition;
```

Here, "table_name" represents the name of the table from which to delete data, and "condition" specifies the criteria for selecting the rows to delete. The WHERE clause is optional, and if omitted, it will delete all rows from the specified table.

For example, the following statement deletes all rows from the "customers" table:

```
DELETE FROM customers;
```

You can use the WHERE clause to delete specific rows based on certain criteria. For instance, the following statement deletes rows from the "customers" table where the "age" column is greater than 30:

```
DELETE FROM customers
WHERE age > 30;
```

The DELETE statement can be combined with other SQL statements, such as JOIN and subqueries, to perform more complex deletions.

Using the DELETE statement with caution is essential, as it permanently removes data from the database. Before executing a DELETE statement, ensure you have a backup of the database and thoroughly understand the consequences of the deletion.

The DELETE statement removes unwanted or outdated data from a database table, ensuring data integrity and accuracy. By utilizing the WHERE clause, users can control which rows to delete, and also combine the statement with other SQL statements for more complex deletion scenarios.

MERGE

The MERGE statement will insert, update, or delete data in one table with data from a second table or a subquery. Some unique ways are needed for semi-structured data to merge. However, once we organize semi-structured data into a table structure, we can use the standard merge function to combine data sourced via semi-structured data.

It offers a powerful method for combining and modifying data in a database.

However, semi-structured data, which does not conform to a predefined schema or structure, presents unique challenges when merging with structured data in a relational database. To effectively merge semi-structured data, organizing and transforming it into a table structure that aligns with the relational model is necessary.

Once the semi-structured data is structured, we can use the standard MERGE function to combine it with data from other sources. This enables seamless integration of diverse data types, allowing for efficient data management and analysis.

The MERGE statement follows a specific syntax that includes the target table, the source table, or subquery and the conditions for determining which rows to insert, update, or delete:

- **Insert Operation:** Inserts new rows into the target table based on data from the source table or subquery.

- **Update Operation:** This operation updates existing rows in the target table based on matching criteria and values provided in the source table or subquery.

- **Delete Operation:** This operation removes rows from the target table that meet specific criteria, such as those not found in the source table or subquery.

The MERGE statement is a versatile and efficient tool for managing data in a relational database, catering to both structured and semi-structured data requirements. By leveraging the MERGE statement effectively, organizations can gain valuable insights from a wide range of data sources, supporting informed decision-making and improving overall data management practices.

DCL

Data Control Language (DCL) commands manage object permissions. Roles and users are created at the account level, and grants are issued at the database, schema, and object levels. Grants cannot be given to users; they are only given to roles. Then, those roles are GRANTed to users. Commands include:

- **GRANT**: Grant a given permission to a particular ROLE or grant a role to a user.

- **REVOKE**: Revoke will remove the access immediately from the ROLE.

TCL

Transaction Control Language (TCL) ensures that data is consistent at a given time. By explicitly starting a transaction during a session, the session tells Snowflake that it is going to Update, Insert, or Delete data. Once the data manipulation process is complete and verified through the testing defined as part of the transaction, the transaction can be either COMMITTED (made permanent) or a ROLLBACK can be issued that will reset the data to its state prior to the BEGIN TRANSACTION command. Commands include:

- **BEGIN TRANSACTION**: Start the Transaction. Once the transaction is started, the data issued during the session should undergo a CRUD operation.

- **COMMIT**: Once it is verified that the data that was supposed to be updated is updated and that the data that was not supposed to be updated was not updated, issuing the COMMIT during the session will make the change permanent.

- **ROLLBACK**: If there is an issue with the update, whether the data that was supposed to be updated was not updated or that data that was not supposed to be updated was updated, the ROLLBACK command will reset the data in the table that was manipulated to its state prior to the BEGIN TRANSACTION command.

Query mechanics

The mechanics of a SELECT statement may differ in each database, but fundamentally, here's what happens.

It starts with parsing. At its heart, a SELECT statement retrieves data from one or more tables in a database. The general structure looks like this:

```
SELECT [DISTINCT] column1, column2, ..., function(column3) AS alias
FROM table1
[JOIN table2 ON condition]
[WHERE condition]
[GROUP BY column1, column2, ...]
[HAVING condition]
[ORDER BY column1 ASC/DESC, column2 ASC/DESC, ...]
[LIMIT number];
```

Let's review these clauses:

- **SELECT:** Specify the columns you want to retrieve. You can use the * wildcard to select all columns. While using the asterisk wildcard is acceptable for illustrative and training purposes, do not use it for any production application. The SQL stored within a production application relies on the order and number of columns within a table. By using a wildcard rather than specifying the columns needed at that point in the application will cause the application to break if there are any changes to the data structure, such as adding metadata columns or columns needed to comply with an external dependency.

- **DISTINCT:** Optionally used to remove duplicate rows from the result set. By definition, a table should only ever have distinct columns because of the nature of the relationship between relational theory and set theory. However, this predicate is needed because of the nature of how the original application captures the data, specifically in the case where a subset of columns is selected. The data should, in theory, be unique for the entire set of rows in a given table. However, in some cases, there will be duplicate rows when selecting only a particular column, such as "LastName" from a table.

- **FROM:** Specifies the table(s) from which data is fetched.

- **JOIN:** Used to combine rows from two or more tables based on a related column between them. Standard join types include INNER JOIN, LEFT JOIN, RIGHT JOIN, and FULL JOIN.

- **ON:** Specifies the condition ON each table and how the tables referenced in the SELECT statement should be related.

- **WHERE:** Filters rows based on a specified condition.

- **GROUP BY:** Groups rows that have the same values into summary rows. Often used with aggregate functions (like SUM, AVG, COUNT, MAX, MIN).

- **HAVING:** Filters the results of the GROUP BY clause.

- **ORDER BY:** Sorts the result set by one or more columns in ascending or descending order.

- **LIMIT:** Restricts the number of rows returned.

Here is an example SELECT with basic clauses:

```
SELECT [DISTINCT] column1, column2, ..., function(column3) AS alias
FROM table1
[JOIN table2 ON condition]
[WHERE condition]
[GROUP BY column1, column2, ...]
[HAVING condition]
[ORDER BY column1 ASC/DESC, column2 ASC/DESC, ...]
[LIMIT number];
```

This query selects specific columns from the employees table, filters for employees with a salary above 50,000, and sorts the results by last name in ascending order.

A SQL parser is a software component that analyzes a SQL query, understands its structure and meaning, and translates it into a format the database engine can execute. The parsing process involves multiple phases:

- **Lexical Analysis:** The parser breaks down the SQL statement into individual tokens (keywords, identifiers, operators, and literals). This is like identifying the words in a sentence.

- **Syntactic Analysis:** The parser checks whether the arrangement of tokens conforms to the SQL grammar rules. This is like checking a sentence's grammatical correctness.

- **Semantic Analysis:** The parser verifies that the query makes logical sense within the context of the database schema. For example, it checks if the referenced tables and columns exist, if data types are compatible, and if the query adheres to any constraints.

- **Query Optimization:** The parser (or a separate optimizer) analyzes the query and determines the most efficient execution. This involves selecting the best join order, utilizing indexes, and rewriting the query to achieve better performance.

- **Query Execution:** The optimized query is translated into low-level instructions that the database engine can understand and execute. This involves fetching data from storage, performing any necessary calculations or filtering, and returning the result set.

SQL parser

A generic SQL parser typically includes the following components:

- **Lexer:** Responsible for lexical analysis, breaking the input query into tokens.

- **Parser:** Implements the syntactic and semantic analysis, building an internal representation of the query (often an Abstract Syntax Tree or AST).

- **Optimizer:** Determines the optimal execution plan for the query.

- **Executor:** Executes the optimized plan against the database, returning the result set.

Let's consider a simple example of processing a SELECT statement:

```
SELECT employee_id, first_name, last_name
FROM employees
WHERE department = 'Sales';
```

- **Lexical analysis:** The lexer identifies tokens like SELECT, employee_id, FROM, employees, WHERE, department, =, and 'Sales.'

- **Syntactic analysis:** The parser ensures that the token arrangement follows the SQL syntax rules for a SELECT statement.

- **Semantic analysis:** The parser verifies that the employees table and the columns employee_id, first_name, last_name, and department exist. It also checks that the department column can be compared to a string value.

- **Query optimization:** The optimizer may choose to use an index on the department column to locate rows that match the condition quickly.

- **Query execution:** The database engine scans the employees' table, possibly using the index, applies the filter condition, and returns the matching rows, projecting only the requested columns.

Challenges with using a SQL parser include:

- **SQL dialects:** Different database systems may have slightly different SQL syntax and features. A generic parser needs to be flexible enough to handle variations.

- **Query complexity:** Complex queries with subqueries, joins, and nested conditions can be challenging to parse and optimize.

- **Performance:** The parser and optimizer need to be efficient to avoid introducing significant overhead in query processing.

CASE statements and aggregation

A CASE statement is a conditional expression within SQL. It allows you to categorize data or perform different calculations based on specific conditions. It's incredibly powerful for grouping and summarizing data when used within an aggregate function. For example:

```
SELECT department,
       COUNT(CASE WHEN salary > 60000 THEN 1 ELSE NULL END) AS
high_earners,
       AVG(salary) AS avg_salary
FROM employees
GROUP BY department
HAVING avg_salary > 55000;
```

In this example:

1. We group employees by department.

2. The CASE statement counts employees earning above 60,000 as "high earners" for each department.

3. We calculate the average salary for each department.

4. The HAVING clause filters out departments with an average salary below 55,000.

Key points

- The order of clauses in a SELECT statement is essential because of how the statement is parsed.

- You can use aliases to give meaningful names to calculated columns or results of functions.

- CASE statements are versatile tools for manipulating and analyzing data within SQL queries.

- Relational databases have extensive capabilities beyond what's covered here. To fully harness their power, explore concepts like subqueries, nested SELECTs, and advanced join techniques.

Since I wrote about relational algebra and relational calculus previously, we should tie these together.

Relational algebra theory

Relational algebra is a procedural query language where you express queries as a sequence of operations on relations (tables). Each operation takes one or more relations as input and produces a new relation as output.

Here is how the SELECT statement relates to relational algebra operations:

- **SELECT:** The SELECT clause corresponds to the Projection (π) operation in relational algebra. It selects specific attributes (columns) from a relation.

- **FROM:** The FROM clause, combined with JOIN, relates to the Cartesian Product ($\times$) and Selection (σ) operations. Cartesian Product creates all combinations of rows from the joined tables, and Selection filters those rows based on the join condition and WHERE clause predicates.

- **WHERE:** The WHERE clause directly maps to the Selection (σ) operation, filtering rows based on a given condition.

- **GROUP BY:** The GROUP BY clause corresponds to the Grouping (γ) operation, which groups rows by the specified attributes.

- **HAVING:** The HAVING clause is another Selection (σ) applied after the Grouping (γ) operation.

- **ORDER BY:** The ORDER BY clause is like the Sorting (τ) operation, arranging rows based on one or more attributes.

Consider the query:

```
SELECT department,
    COUNT(CASE WHEN salary > 60000 THEN 1 ELSE NULL END) AS
high_earners,
    AVG(salary) AS avg_salary
FROM employees
GROUP BY department
HAVING avg_salary > 55000;
```

In relational algebra, we express this as:

π department, avg_salary (σ avg_salary > 60000 (γ department; AVG(salary)$\rightarrow$avg_salary (σ salary > 50000 (employees))))

Relational calculus theory

Relational calculus is a declarative query language where you describe the desired result without specifying how to obtain it. There are two main types:

- **Tuple Relational Calculus (TRC):** In TRC, you define a query by specifying a condition that tuples (rows) must satisfy. The SELECT statement is closely related to TRC as it essentially describes the set of tuples that meet the specified conditions in the WHERE, GROUP BY, and HAVING clauses.

- **Domain Relational Calculus (DRC):** In DRC, you express queries in terms of attributes (columns) rather than tuples. While SQL doesn't directly mirror DRC, the concepts of selecting and filtering based on attribute values are fundamental to both.

Relational algebra and calculus key takeaways

- SQL's SELECT statement is a practical implementation of relational algebra and relational calculus concepts.

- Relational algebra focuses on the procedural steps involved in query execution, while relational calculus focuses on the declarative description of the desired result.

- Understanding the theoretical underpinnings helps you grasp the underlying logic of SQL queries and optimize their performance.

The previous section covers lots of the details of a SELECT clause, but the TL;DR summary is:

When we execute a query, the database engine will parse the query, do all the things overviewed above, and start doing what the query tells the engine to do. Once we are past all the parsing, lexing, and optimization, the function processing begins.

```
Select LastName,count(*) from customers where LastName like 'A%'
group by LastName;
```

For example, in the above query, indexes are used to identify the records with the correct LastName value when the table is read. Then, all those rows of data are passed to the group by function—all of them—at the same time. This will return sets of records with the same last name as column one. The result of the group by statement will be passed to the count() function, which will count the number of records in each logical group identified by the unique last name.

Clauses and functions

The clauses associated with the Select statement are the focus here.

The SELECT statement has several essential clauses to use to refine the results and perform various operations on the data. These clauses include:

- **GROUP BY**: The GROUP BY clause groups the rows of the result set based on one or more columns. This allows users to perform aggregate *functions* (such as SUM, COUNT, AVG, etc.) on the grouped data, summarizing and analyzing the results.

- **ORDER BY**: The ORDER BY clause sorts the rows of the result set based on one or more columns. This allows users to organize and present the data in a specific order, making it easier to identify patterns and trends.

- **JOIN**: The JOIN clause combines rows from two or more tables based on a common column or columns. This allows users to simultaneously establish relationships between tables and retrieve data from multiple sources. There are several types of joins, such as inner, outer, and cross, each with its specific functionality.

- **WHERE**: The WHERE clause filters the rows of the result set based on a specified condition. This allows users to restrict the data returned by the SELECT statement, focusing only on the rows that meet the specified criteria. The WHERE clause can be used with various comparison operators (=, <>, >, <, >=, <=) and logical operators (AND, OR, NOT) to construct complex filtering conditions.

In the select statement section, I explained that the SELECT statement consistently produces a data structure similar to a table's definition. The header rows returned by the SELECT statement are structurally the same as the table definitions used in a create table command. The rows returned are the same types of rows we would see residing on disk in the table structure.

The mechanics of how the SELECT statement works are an implementation detail for each database compliant with the SQL standard. We covered the conceptual details in the section on query mechanics. A couple of things to remember:

- A SELECT clause will ALWAYS return a table-like structure.

- A function will be applied to all rows at the same time in the select portion of the query.

- The function can be sophisticated, and parse out large objects stored in columns.

- The functions that do parsing of non-trivial embedded data structures are the functions that parse and extract data from either XML or JSON.

When we combine structured data with semi-structured data, the functions will do the heavy lifting.

Structured and semi-structured data

Database professionals tend to refer to data in tables as structured. This structure comes from the original definition of the relation. A relation is a tuple of items from a set of attributes (columns) related to some defined key.

A relational database is a type of database that organizes data into one or more tables, where each table consists of rows and columns. Relational databases are widely used to manage structured data, which is data organized in a specific and predefined way, such as in a table with fixed columns. However, relational databases can also handle semi-structured data, which is data that does not have a fixed structure but still has some organization to it. Let's explore the similarities and differences between structured and semi-structured data from a relational database perspective.

While some debate exists about using the term semi-structured when it comes to objects, we will see shortly XML and JSON have some structure. The differentiation for me is the use of predicates. Predicate-based and non-predicate-based data may sound confusing, but going back to the fundamental definitions of our relations, the predicate is a key differentiator. A relation in a database is predicate-based. Each individual value in a "column" is a predicate that is an enhanced attribute of the primary key. Nothing in an XML or JSON document is a predicate. Since a relational table consists of individual predicates, even if multiple tables are joined together, creating a hierarchy or nesting all predicates enriches understanding of the primary keys associated with each relation. Conversely, a document has a variable structure, not isolated to an individual key.

Structured data is data organized in a specific and predefined way. Structured data is typically stored in a relational database as a table with a fixed number of columns and a fixed data type for each column. For example, a table that stores customer information may have columns for customer name, address, phone number, and email address. Each column has a specific data type, such as string, integer, or date, and each row in the table represents a single customer with values in each column that correspond to their name, address, phone number, and email address. Structured data is easy to query and analyze because it has a fixed structure that can be easily understood and is consistent across all rows in the table.

Semi-structured data, on the other hand, does not require a fixed structure but still has some organization. We typically store semi-structured data in a relational database as unstructured data, such as a blob or a text field, or in a specialized semi-structured data store. Examples of semi-structured data include XML documents, JSON files, and log files. Semi-structured data is more flexible than structured data because it can have a variable structure that can change over time. However, semi-structured data is more difficult to query and analyze because it may have a nested or hierarchical structure that requires specialized tools or techniques to access and analyze.

One similarity between structured and semi-structured data is that we can store both in a relational database. Relational databases are designed to handle structured data, but can also handle semi-structured data by storing it in an unstructured data field or a specialized semi-structured data store. This allows organizations to store all their data in a single database, simplifying data management and reducing the need for multiple data stores.

Another similarity between structured and semi-structured data is that we can query both types of data using SQL. SQL is designed to work with structured data. However, SQL can also be used to query semi-structured data by using specialized *functions* and *operators* that can extract data from nested or hierarchical structures. This allows organizations to use the same tools and techniques to query structured and semi-structured data, simplifying data analysis and reducing the need for specialized tools.

Despite these similarities, there are also several differences between structured and semi-structured data from a relational database perspective. One major difference is that structured data has a fixed structure, while semi-structured data has a variable structure. So, we can easily query and analyze structured data using standard SQL techniques, while semi-structured data requires specialized techniques to access and analyze.

Another difference is that structured data is typically easier to validate and enforce data integrity. Structured data has a fixed number of columns with a fixed data type for each column. Since semi-structured data does not leverage the capability of predicates, the integrity of data within a document itself can vary greatly. XML and JSON do not have a built-in way of ensuring data integrity between different sections of the data. App divas write code to ensure that the data in a document is "correct" by their isolated self-referential definition.

Ingestion

The Snowflake variant data type is a flexible data type that can store semi-structured data in a column of a table in Snowflake. It can store unstructured, semi-structured, or structured data in a single column, such as JSON, XML, Avro, Parquet, or ORC data formats. We can use the Snowflake variant data type to store complex data structures that do not fit well into traditional relational database tables.

Using the Snowflake variant data type, you can store data with different attributes and structures in a single column. For example, you can store JSON data that contains multiple key-value pairs or nested data structures. You can also store data in a hierarchical format, such as XML, or store data in a compressed format, such as Avro, Parquet, or ORC.

To use the Snowflake variant data type, you must create a table with a column with the variant data type. You can then insert data into the table using SQL statements. You can also use Snowflake's built-in functions to query and manipulate the data stored in the variant column.

The Snowflake variant data type is particularly useful when storing unstructured data to use later in views. By storing unstructured data in a variant column, you can easily query and extract the data using SQL, and then transform the data into a structured format to use with views. This allows you to take advantage of Snowflake's powerful data warehousing capabilities while still working with unstructured data.

XML

XML, or Extensible Markup Language, is a cornerstone in data representation and exchange. Its versatility, human-readability, and structured format have solidified its role in various applications across industries and domains.

The roots of XML can be traced back to the 1960s, when IBM developed the Generalized Markup Language (GML). This early markup language laid the foundation for the Standard Generalized Markup Language (SGML), standardized in 1986. SGML's complexity and focus on document publishing paved the way for a more straightforward, more adaptable markup language—XML.

In 1996, the World Wide Web Consortium (W3C) formed a working group to develop XML, led by Jon Bosak of Sun Microsystems. The goal was to create a markup language that was both human-readable and machine-readable, and capable of representing structured data across different platforms and applications. The first version of XML was released in 1998, marking a significant step towards a more flexible and accessible approach to data representation.

XML employs a hierarchical structure consisting of elements, attributes, and text content. Elements are defined using tags enclosed in angle brackets (e.g., <element>) and can contain other elements, attributes, or text. Attributes provide additional information about elements and are specified within the opening tag (e.g., <element attribute="value">). Text content represents the actual data within an element.

This structured format facilitates the representation of complex data relationships. For instance, an XML document representing a book might contain elements for the title, author, publisher, and chapters, each with their respective attributes and text content.

XML data can be captured and represented through various methods. Manual creation involves writing XML code directly using a text editor. Automated generation leverages software tools or APIs to convert data from other formats (e.g., databases, spreadsheets) into XML. Web forms can also capture user input and generate corresponding XML data.

XML's adaptability has led to its adoption in numerous applications, including:

- **Data exchange:** XML serves as a common format for exchanging data between different systems and applications. Its platform independence and self-describing nature facilitate seamless integration.

- **Web services:** XML plays a crucial role in web services, enabling communication and data exchange between distributed systems over the internet. SOAP (Simple Object Access Protocol) and REST (Representational State Transfer) often utilize XML for message formatting.

- **Configuration Files:** Many software applications employ XML-based configuration files to store settings and preferences. The structured format allows for easy modification and parsing.

- **Document Markup:** XML's roots in SGML make it well-suited for document markup. XHTML (Extensible HyperText Markup Language), an XML-based successor to HTML, demonstrates its use in web page structuring.

- **APIs:** APIs (Application Programming Interfaces) can use XML for request and response formatting.

This enables developers to interact with web services and retrieve data in a structured manner.

- **Kafka:** Kafka, a distributed streaming platform, can handle XML data as messages. This facilitates real-time data processing and integration across various systems.

We can store XML data in various ways, each with its advantages:

- **File systems:** XML documents can be stored as files on a file system. This approach is simple but it does not have the more advanced search and querying capabilities.

- **Databases:** Relational databases can store XML data in specialized columns or tables. This enables structured querying and indexing, but complex XML structures may require additional processing.

- **Document-oriented databases:** Document-oriented databases, like MongoDB, are designed to store and retrieve semi-structured data, including XML. They offer flexibility and scalability for handling diverse data formats.

XML's legacy as a versatile and adaptable markup language continues to thrive in the digital age. Its structured format, human readability, and platform independence have cemented its role in data exchange, web services, configuration files, document markup, and numerous other applications. As technology evolves, XML's ability to represent and exchange data clearly and concisely ensures its relevance for years to come.

We will first discuss the various specialized XML functions built into the Snowflake parsing engine. Next, we will discuss how XML structures can be created from relational tables.

The first step in parsing and extracting XML data is to load it into a Snowflake table using the COPY INTO command. Once the XML data has been loaded into a table, we can parse and extract it using the various XML functions built into the Snowflake parsing engine. Let's say we have an XML document containing information about the United States Presidents until 1900. The XML document might look something like this:

```xml
<?xml version="1.0" encoding="UTF-8"?>
<Presidents>
  <President>
    <Name>George Washington</Name>
    <TermStart>1789</TermStart>
    <TermEnd>1797</TermEnd>
  </President>
  <President>
    <Name>John Adams</Name>
    <TermStart>1797</TermStart>
    <TermEnd>1801</TermEnd>
  </President>
</Presidents>
```

We can then use a few parser functions to shred this XML document into a relational table. The following SQL query shows how to do this:

```
with presidents_xml as (
SELECT parse_xml('<?xml version="1.0" encoding="UTF-8"?>
<Presidents>
  <President>
    <Name>George Washington</Name>
    <TermStart>1789</TermStart>
    <TermEnd>1797</TermEnd>
  </President>
  <President>
    <Name>John Adams</Name>
    <TermStart>1797</TermStart>
    <TermEnd>1801</TermEnd>
  </President>
  </Presidents>
')::variant as xml_object
)
select
XMLGET( president.value, 'Name' ):"$"::String as Name,
XMLGET( president.value, 'TermStart' ):"$"::String as TermStart,
XMLGET( president.value, 'TermEnd' ):"$"::String as TermEnd
from
presidents_xml,
lateral FLATTEN(presidents_xml.xml_object:"$") president
 where GET( president.value, '@') = 'President';
```

This query will produce the following output:

Name	TermStart	TermEnd
George Washington	1789	1797
John Adams	1797	1801
...	...	...

Step by step, let us walk through what is happening here.

The CTE (Common Table Expression) is:

```
with presidents_xml as (
SELECT parse_xml('<?xml version="1.0" encoding="UTF-8"?>
<Presidents>
  <President>
    <Name>George Washington</Name>
    <TermStart>1789</TermStart>
    <TermEnd>1797</TermEnd>
  </President>
  <President>
    <Name>John Adams</Name>
    <TermStart>1797</TermStart>
    <TermEnd>1801</TermEnd>
  </President>
  </Presidents>
')::variant as xml_object
)
```

Without doing any more complicated loading of XML data into a variant column in an existing table, I simply defined the table presidents_xml as a table with one column of data type variant named xml_object. This parse_xml function converts the string of the XML "document" into an actual XML object that can be used in later processing.

Before covering the part of the query that creates the table object output, we have to jump down to the from clause:

```
from
presidents_xml,
lateral FLATTEN(presidents_xml.xml_object:"$") president
 where GET( president.value, '@') = 'President';
```

The FLATTEN function explodes compound values into multiple rows and treats the result as a table. So, the xml_object defined in the CTE now becomes multiple rows of data that are still XML.

The lateral command tells the parser to join the previous table with the upcoming table, which can be a subquery or a non-standard entity like an XML or JSON object.

```
XMLGET( president.value, 'Name' ):"$"::String as name,
XMLGET( president.value, 'TermStart' ):"$"::String as TermStart,
XMLGET( president.value, 'TermEnd' ):"$"::String as TermEnd
```

The XMLGET function's first parameter is the value from the FLATTEN command; this says to GET the named value of the specified second parameter from the object that is defined as the first parameter.

The:"$" portion is formatting, telling the command to return the values without the XML tag that defines the value portion we are referencing. Finally, the::String command says to format the data that is returned as a string.

Let's say we have a relational table that contains information about the Presidents of the United States up until 1900. The table might look something like this:

Name	TermStart	TermEnd
George Washington	1789	1797
John Adams	1797	1801
...	...	...

We can use the TO_XML, OBJECT_CONSTRUCT, and ARRAY_AGG functions to create an XML document from this table.

The following SQL query shows how to do this:

```sql
with presidents_xml as (
SELECT parse_xml('<?xml version="1.0" encoding="UTF-8"?>
<Presidents>
  <President>
    <Name>George Washington</Name>
    <TermStart>1789</TermStart>
    <TermEnd>1797</TermEnd>
  </President>
  <President>
    <Name>John Adams</Name>
    <TermStart>1797</TermStart>
    <TermEnd>1801</TermEnd>
  </President>
  </Presidents>
')::variant as xml_object
), base_table as (
select
XMLGET( president.value, 'Name' ):"$"::String as name,
XMLGET( president.value, 'TermStart' ):"$"::String as TermStart,
XMLGET( president.value, 'TermEnd' ):"$"::String as TermEnd
from
presidents_xml,
lateral FLATTEN(presidents_xml.xml_object:"$") president
```

```
where GET( president.value, '@') = 'President'
)
select
to_xml(
  object_construct('Presidents',
    array_agg(
      object_construct('President',
        object_construct('Name',name,
                'TermStart',TermStart,
                'TermEnd',TermEnd
        )
      )
    )
  )
  ) as XML_OBJECT
from base_table;
```

This query will produce the following output:

```
<SnowflakeData type="OBJECT">

<Presidents type="ARRAY">

<e type="OBJECT">

<President type="OBJECT">

<Name type="VARCHAR">George Washington</Name>

<TermEnd type="VARCHAR">1797</TermEnd>

<TermStart type="VARCHAR">1789</TermStart>

</President></e>

<e type="OBJECT">
```

```
<President type="OBJECT">

<Name type="VARCHAR">John Adams</Name>

<TermEnd type="VARCHAR">1801</TermEnd>

<TermStart type="VARCHAR">1797</TermStart>

</President>

</e>

</Presidents>

</SnowflakeData>
```

The only actual complicated portion of the query is the OBJECT_CONSTRUCT and ARRAY_AGG functions.

Using the first query that converts XML data into a relational structure, we can expand that query following the capabilities of the WITH clause that creates an in memory table. Wrapping the first queries output into a CTE (Common Table Expression) called base_table gives us a relational structure to work with.

The last section of the query converts the base_table CTE into an XML document.

The OBJECT_CONSTRUCT function constructs objects from the data per row. Here, we want an object of the name President with the values of Name, TermEnd, and TermStart. Since we are bringing all these rows together into a single XML structure, we use the ARRAY_AGG function to create an aggregate array of all the objects.

Finally, we do another OBJECT_CONSTRUCT to create a single Presidents object and convert that to an XML object using TO_XML.[24]

The TO_XML function generates some additional tags, as covered in the documentation.

By understanding how to parse and extract XML data and how to create XML structures from relational tables, you can use Snowflake to unlock the full potential of your XML data.

JSON

The need for a standardized, lightweight, and human-readable data interchange format has become increasingly apparent in the ever-evolving digital communication landscape. This demand led to the emergence of JSON (JavaScript Object Notation), a format that has revolutionized how we represent and exchange data across various platforms and applications.

JSON evolved from the limitations of XML (eXtensible Markup Language), which was widely used for data interchange in the early 2000s. While powerful, XML was often lengthy and cumbersome, making it less suitable for real-time web applications and resource-constrained environments.

---

[24] https://docs.snowflake.com/en/sql-reference/functions/to_xml

Douglas Crockford, a renowned JavaScript programmer, recognized the need for a simpler and more efficient alternative. He leveraged the object syntax of JavaScript, a language rapidly gaining popularity at the time, and devised a format that was easy to understand and parse.

In 2001, Crockford registered the domain name json.org and published the first JSON specification. The simplicity and elegance of JSON resonated with developers, leading to its rapid adoption across various web technologies.

JSON data is structured as a collection of key-value pairs, where keys are strings and values of various types, including Strings, Numbers, Booleans, arrays, and even nested JSON objects. This hierarchical structure enables the representation of complex data relationships concisely and organized for a single bespoke application.

For example, consider a JSON object representing a person:

```
{
  "name": "John Doe",
  "age": 30,
  "isStudent": false,
  "address": {
    "street": "123 Main St",
    "city": "Anytown",
    "state": "CA",
    "zip": "12345"
  },
  "phoneNumbers": [
    { "type": "home", "number": "555-555-1212" },
    { "type": "work", "number": "555-555-1213" }
  ]
}
```

This example shows how JSON can capture various data types, including nested objects (address) and arrays (phoneNumbers).

JSON's versatility has led to its widespread adoption in many use cases spanning different domains and technologies.

- **APIs (Application Programming Interfaces)**: JSON has become the de facto standard for data exchange in web APIs. Its lightweight nature and compatibility with various programming languages make it ideal for transmitting data between client-side applications and server-side services.

- **Kafka**: In the realm of event-driven architectures, Kafka, a distributed streaming platform, often utilizes JSON to serialize and transmit messages between producers and consumers. JSON's schema-less nature allows unruly message structures, accommodating evolving data requirements.

- **Configuration files**: JSON's human-readable format and hierarchical structure make it well-suited for configuration files. Many modern software applications and frameworks leverage JSON to store and manage configuration settings, providing an intuitive and easily adaptable format.

- **Document type storage**: NoSQL "databases", such as MongoDB and CouchDB, often store data in JSON-like documents. This approach enables flexible schema design and facilitates the storage of semi-structured or unstructured data. Since these engines are not based on predicates, consistency or integrity is not required.

We can store JSON data in various ways, depending on the specific use case and storage technology. In file systems, JSON data is typically stored in plain text files with the .json extension. In databases, JSON data might be embedded within larger documents or stored as separate JSON objects.

JSON has emerged as a cornerstone of modern data interchange, offering a simple, efficient, and versatile format for capturing and representing data. Its widespread adoption across diverse technologies and use cases is a testament to its effectiveness in facilitating seamless communication and data exchange in the digital age. As technology continues to advance, JSON is poised to remain a vital tool for developers and organizations seeking to harness the power of data.

In the realm of modern data management, the seamless interplay between structured and semi-structured data has become paramount. Snowflake empowers organizations to navigate this landscape with finesse.

Before we embark on our journey through Snowflake's JSON capabilities, let's establish a foundational understanding of JSON data itself. JSON, short for JavaScript Object Notation, is a lightweight, text-based format for representing structured data. It's characterized by its human-readable syntax and widespread adoption across diverse domains, from web APIs to configuration files.

At its core, JSON data contains key-value pairs, where keys are strings, and values can be strings, numbers, booleans, arrays, objects, or null. This hierarchical structure allows for the representation of complex relationships and nested data elements, making JSON a versatile choice for many applications.

Snowflake's prowess in handling JSON data stems from its ability to seamlessly parse and extract information from JSON documents through specific functions, transforming them into a tabular representation that aligns with traditional relational database structures. This transformation enables analysts and data scientists to leverage the full spectrum of Snowflake's query and analytical capabilities when working with JSON data.

At the heart of Snowflake's JSON parsing engine lies a set of specialized functions meticulously designed to navigate the intricacies of JSON structures. These functions provide the tools necessary to extract specific values, traverse nested objects and arrays, and reshape JSON data to fit the desired analytical schema.

To illustrate the concepts and techniques we'll explore in this essay, let's consider a hypothetical table named signers that stores information about the Declaration of Independence signers. This table might contain columns such as name, state, profession, and signature_date.

Within the signers table, let's imagine a column named additional_info that holds JSON data containing supplementary details about each signer. This JSON data might include information about their birthdate, place of birth, education, and notable accomplishments.

Snowflake equips users with an array of specialized JSON functions that empower them to extract, transform, and analyze JSON data with precision and flexibility. These functions form the cornerstone of Snowflake's JSON parsing capabilities, enabling the seamless integration of semi-structured data into the analytical workflow.

- **PARSE_JSON**: The PARSE_JSON function serves as the gateway to Snowflake's JSON parsing engine. It accepts a string containing JSON data as input and returns a variant data type representing the parsed JSON structure. This variant data type acts as a container for the JSON data, preserving its hierarchical organization and enabling further manipulation using other JSON functions.

- **GET_PATH**: The GET_PATH function allows for extracting specific values from within a JSON structure. It accepts a JSON variant and a path expression as input and returns the value located at the specified path. The path expression utilizes dot notation to navigate nested objects and arrays, providing a concise and intuitive way to pinpoint desired data elements.

- **GET**: The GET function offers a simplified approach to extracting values from JSON data. It accepts a JSON variant and a key as input and returns the value associated with the specified key. While GET is less versatile than GET_PATH in handling nested structures, it excels in scenarios where the target value resides at the top level of the JSON object.

- **FLATTEN**: The FLATTEN function plays a pivotal role in transforming nested JSON arrays into a tabular format. It accepts a JSON variant containing an array as input and returns a table where each row corresponds to an element within the array. This transformation enables the seamless integration of nested JSON data into SQL queries and analytical operations.

- **LATERAL FLATTEN**: The LATERAL FLATTEN function extends FLATTEN's capabilities by allowing for the flattening of multiple nested arrays within a single JSON structure. It accepts a JSON variant and multiple path expressions as input and returns a table where each row represents a combination of elements from the flattened arrays. This functionality proves invaluable when dealing with complex JSON hierarchies containing multiple levels of nesting.

- **OBJECT_AGG**: The OBJECT_AGG function facilitates the aggregation of key-value pairs into a JSON object. It accepts two columns as input – one representing keys and the other representing values – and returns a JSON object where the keys and values are paired accordingly. This function proves helpful in scenarios where you need to construct JSON objects from relational data.

- **ARRAY_AGG**: The ARRAY_AGG function enables the aggregation of values into a JSON array. It accepts a single column as input and returns a JSON array containing the aggregated values. This function finds application in scenarios where you need to group data and represent the grouped values as a JSON array.

Some of these functions we have already discussed when covering the topic of XML. I will elaborate the query to have some more CTE's and convert the XML data to JSON so we can see how this functionality works with both.

Let's revisit our presidents table and explore how Snowflake's JSON functions can extract specific information from the JSON object column.

- To retrieve the same output of the presidents JSON as if it were like the XML data described previously, here is one query that will do so.

```
SELECT
        j.value:President:Name::STRING as Name,
        j.value:President:TermStart::STRING as TermStart,
        j.value:President:TermEnd::STRING as TermEnd
FROM
        TABLE(FLATTEN(INPUT =>

        parse_json('

        {"Presidents": [

            {"President": {
                        "Name": "George Washington",
                            "TermEnd": "1797",
                            "TermStart": "1789"
```

```
                              }
                    },
                    {"President": {
                         "Name": "John Adams",
                                "TermEnd": "1801",
                                "TermStart": "1797"
                                }
                    }
                    ]
        }')

        , PATH => 'Presidents')

    ) j
```

Snowflake has boatloads of syntactic sugar to make it easy to work with the semi-structured data world.

As we saw earlier, the FLATTEN statement flattens down semi-structured data into a format that is more conducive to work with the SQL statements. SQL only works with table structures as defined originally by Codd and Date. Shoehorning other types of data into this set-based approach could be a daunting task if it were not for the engineers behind the scenes making these functions available for the rest of us to use, these queries would be much more complicated. The PATH option to the function shows that we want to look at all of the elements under the array defined as "Presidents".

Once the JSON data is flattened, it is treated as a table, hence the TABLE function, which transforms string literal data into a table structure that conforms to the SQL standards.

Now that we have a table structure to work with using the TABLE and FLATTEN functions, let us look at the SELECT clause.

As with any troubleshooting technique, I encourage you to take it a step at a time if you want to understand what is happening. The "j" is the alias of the table defined through the previous functions.

"J.value" tells the parser to work with the "value" column of the table "j".

The single colon references the name of the JSON key that we want to retrieve. As you can see from the definition of the JSON data, the key of President is listed twice. However, since this block of JSON contains two different entities, the query will return two rows.

In our case, we want to have two rows, broken into the columns of "Name", "TermStart", and "TermEnd" to match what we have seen before.

Each row has a "President" array. That array consists of the President's full name, the start of their term, and the end of their term. By specifying the full JSON path of the item we want to retrieve and then specifying an Alias for that attribute, we are able to shoehorn the semi-structured JSON data into data that looks, acts, and performs like a table.

If we choose to, we could wrap this statement in a CTE, and use its output as the input to a follow up query. The options seem like they will never end.

If we wanted to transform XML data to JSON we can do a tiny tweak to the SELECT statement from the section on XML.

```
WITH presidents_xml AS (
SELECT
        parse_xml('<?xml version="1.0" encoding="UTF-8"?>
<Presidents>
  <President>
    <Name>George Washington</Name>
    <TermStart>1789</TermStart>
    <TermEnd>1797</TermEnd>
  </President>
  <President>
    <Name>John Adams</Name>
    <TermStart>1797</TermStart>
    <TermEnd>1801</TermEnd>
  </President>
  </Presidents>
')::VARIANT AS xml_object
),
base_table AS (
SELECT
        XMLGET( president.value,'Name' ):"$"::STRING AS Name,
        XMLGET( president.value,'TermStart' ):"$"::STRING AS TermStart,
        XMLGET( president.value,'TermEnd' ):"$"::STRING AS TermEnd
FROM
        presidents_xml,
        LATERAL FLATTEN(presidents_xml.xml_object:"$") president
WHERE
        GET( president.value, '@') = 'President'
),
json_table AS (
SELECT
        to_json(object_construct('Presidents',
    array_agg(
      object_construct('President',
```

```
        object_construct('Name', NAME,
                'TermStart', TermStart,
                'TermEnd', TermEnd
        )
      )
     )
    )
 ) AS json_object
 FROM
          base_table
 )
 SELECT
        *
 FROM
          json_table;
```

In the tapestry of modern data management, the ability to seamlessly parse, extract, transform, and generate JSON data has become indispensable. With its robust JSON parsing engine and specialized functions, Snowflake empowers organizations to navigate the complexities of semi-structured data with finesse.

From extracting specific values to flattening nested arrays, from creating JSON objects to validating JSON schemas, Snowflake offers a comprehensive toolkit for harnessing the potential of JSON data within the analytical ecosystem. By bridging the gap between structured and semi-structured data paradigms, Snowflake enables organizations to unlock valuable insights and drive data-driven decision-making from a single platform.

As we've journeyed through the intricacies of Snowflake's JSON capabilities, we've witnessed how this cloud-based data warehousing platform empowers users to seamlessly integrate, analyze, and transform JSON data, fostering a new era of data agility and innovation. Whether you're working with web APIs, IoT sensor data, or any other source of semi-structured information, Snowflake provides the tools and functionalities necessary to extract meaningful insights and drive business success.

In the ever-evolving data management landscape, Snowflake stands as a beacon of innovation. It illuminates the path toward a future where structured and semi-structured data coexist harmoniously, fueling a new generation of analytical possibilities.

This is a very tiny section in this overall book, but the importance of understanding the process of how SQL treats everything as a table, leverages functions within the context of set-based processing, parses additional data structures not previously defined to the database engine, and other powerful capabilities must be understood. In my experience too many application developers do not know what is happening within the SQL lexer, parser, executor, and optimizer. Because they lack this fundamental knowledge, they try to "help" the database by writing additional unnecessary code that makes things more complicated. This also extends into the worlds of data science, business science, data analytics, and similar approaches.

This is set processing. A function is being passed *to* a set of data. The function is applied to the entire recordset—not one row at a time, not in a cursor, and not sequentially. Simultaneously, the function is applied to the data for every record in memory. Within the past few years, a conversation began about taking the processing to the data rather than having the data come to the processing. A sophisticated database engine will take the processing to the data, and this is done out of the box. Only recently has more sophisticated processing become available in most databases to leverage this set of processing capabilities.

This is one of the reasons why the performance of relational databases is light speed, or, dare I say, ludicrous speed, beyond application code.[25] This is also why the performance of relational databases will always be fundamentally faster than any document-type database. Because the document-type database processes a single document at a time, a relational database will process millions, if not billions, of rows in memory to provide the result of the function that is running in memory. That function could be a count, sum, case statement, average, or any mathematical or user-defined function.

> *When I hear complaints about SQL performance, my first answer is that we need to look into what the developer is doing wrong.*

Chances are they do not understand the capabilities of the powerful engine at their fingertips. Since SQL is usually a secondary consideration to application developers, this lack of understanding necessary to perform a SQL statement adequately will cause runaway costs, projects to run over time, and many other adverse outcomes. Since most application programming books I have read cover little when it comes to data, they essentially say something

---

[25] https://www.youtube.com/watch?v=ygE01sOhzz0&t=18s

like: "put your SELECT * query here", then as the data scales, the application performance begins to dive. There is so much more to the proper performance of a Select statement than arbitrarily building an index.

If an 18th-century sailor were to be put in charge of a 21st-century destroyer, they would wreck the ship. The capabilities of the modern database engine require more than passive interest to do things properly. Data Structures should be organized properly. Queries should be optimized and adjusted based on well-formed reusable Data Structures.

When all other factors are equal, SQL statements consistently outperform application code in terms of data processing. This underscores SQL's efficiency and speed in handling large volumes of data.

Now, let us dive into why a well-done database will perform an order of magnitude better than anything that an application developer can put together to attempt to duplicate the SQL engine's capabilities.

SQL in Set Builder Notation

Now that we've covered the important foundational topics, let's synthesize these diverse concepts together. The goal in bringing these things together is ultimately to be able to apply the ability to leverage quantifiable methods to building and supporting an enrichment platform, create data products, and ultimately make the data of the organization do more work based on the structures that are built in which the data is stored.

During the evolution of relational theory, a language was developed to accurately define the workings of all the definitions. This language, which is either wrapped in relational algebra or relational calculus, plays a crucial role in specifying the correct functioning of relational databases. This language is esoteric and is specific to either relational algebra or relational calculus—and it is not SQL.

In later sections of this book, we will cover mathematical transformations where the source is a relation or table.

Relational algebra has a syntax written to explain how the language works. The symbols are σ,π,×,∪,∩, and -. I showed how these work in the section on relational algebra.

To reduce language complexity and cognitive shifts, let's write at least some basic Select statements in more generic set theory notation. I am choosing not to use the relational algebra notation to keep things as simple and purely mathematical as possible. Here is an example of my attempt to translate SQL to set notation.

SQL:

```
Select FirstName,LastName,Address from Person where LastName = 'Smith'
```

Set notation:

$$x_1, x_2, x_3 : x_i \in P, 1 \leq i \leq 3, x_3 =' Smith'$$

In other words, this means to retrieve the columns $x_1, x_2,$ and x_3 from the set of all columns x_i that exist in the relation Person (P) where the index i is an integer less than or equal to 1 and less than or equal to 3, where the contents of the column x_3 is equal to the text "Smith".

I will convert only a few SQL statements to set theory in this book. Given that it can be done with one select statement, then the set theory notation can only become more complicated as the select statement becomes more complicated.

Graph Theory

"The origins of graph theory are humble, even frivolous." -
Norman L. Biggs

Graph theory is a formal, abstract way to study how three
or more things are related and what impact this relationship
has on each of the individual things.

Some terms that are unique to Graph Theory should be
defined before they are used in the rest of this chapter.

A Vertex, or Node is simply an item that the Graph is
representing. In our case, we will be talking about a Data
Structure (a table) as a vertex.

An Edge is a line drawn between two Vertices that shows
they are related or connected.

A Path is a set of edges between multiple vertices that
shows how to get from one Vertex through one or more
others to ultimately arrive at a final Vertex.

Like many others, I first heard of graph theory in the context of Google.[26] I read a few blogs and thought the topic interesting, but I felt I would never use it. During my self-directed mathematical education, I audited an online course on social network analysis through Coursera. To this day, I still remember hearing the instructor say something that shot through my brain to a memory I had from my days in the Marine Corps learning about database design.

She said: "If you have a set of vertices that you are connecting on paper, and you cannot connect edges between two vertices *without crossing a previous edge*, then you have a non-planar graph."

I immediately stopped the video. Again, I had one of those epiphany moments that showed me how the things I had been doing were related to mathematics.

Before I explain this epiphany, I need to give a little background on graph theory. Graph theory is a branch of mathematics that studies graphs, which are mathematical structures used to model interconnected (related) objects. These objects, called vertices or nodes, are connected by edges or links. Graph theory started with the famous problem of the Seven Bridges of Königsberg, which played a pivotal role in its development.

In the early 18th century, the city of Königsberg in Prussia (now Kaliningrad, Russia) had seven bridges connecting its four landmasses. The people of Königsberg wondered if it was possible to take a walk around the city, crossing each

---

[26] https://en.wikipedia.org/wiki/PageRank`

bridge exactly once and returning to the starting point. Mathematician Leonhard Euler, considered the father of graph theory, tackled this problem and found that it was not possible. Euler's solution involved representing the problem graphically, using nodes and edges, thus giving birth to the concept of a graph.

Euler's work on the Seven Bridges of Königsberg problem laid the foundation for modern graph theory. Over the years, numerous mathematicians and researchers have made significant contributions to the field, further expanding its scope and applications. Here are some key milestones:

- **Eulerian and Hamiltonian paths**: After Euler's initial work, other mathematicians explored paths that traversed all edges of a graph. Eulerian paths visit each edge exactly once, while Hamiltonian paths visit each vertex exactly once. These concepts raised interesting questions about the existence and properties of such paths in several types of graphs.

- **Planar graphs and graph coloring**: Mathematicians studied the properties of graphs that can be drawn on a plane without any edges crossing. These graphs are known as planar graphs. Researchers like Arthur Cayley and Alfred Kempe made essential contributions to understanding planar graphs and the concept of graph coloring, where vertices are assigned colors such that no two adjacent vertices share the same color.

- **Trees and networks:** Graph theory gained wider recognition with the study of trees, which are acyclic-connected graphs. Trees have applications in computer science, optimization algorithms, and network analysis. The concept of spanning trees and minimum spanning trees, pioneered by mathematicians like Otakar Borůvka and Joseph Kruskal, became fundamental in network design and optimization problems.

- **Directed graphs and algorithms:** The study of directed graphs, where edges have a specific direction, led to the development of algorithms and concepts such as shortest path algorithms (Dijkstra's algorithm) and network flow analysis (Ford-Fulkerson algorithm). These algorithms have applications in transportation, communication networks, and computer science.

- **Graphs in computer science:** Graph theory found extensive applications in computer science, particularly in areas like database management systems, graph databases, social network analysis, and graph algorithms. The ability to represent complex relationships and dependencies using graphs has been instrumental in solving various computational problems efficiently.

Now that we have a few definitions related to graph theory before I give a better example of a Data Model, I will connect the two concepts of Graph Theory and Data Modeling.

I had many teachers when it came to data modeling. They all had different takes on various aspects of building a data model. One consistent message, however, was:

"Always try to draw a data model *where no lines cross*. If you must cross the lines, that area of your data model will be more complicated than the other areas."

The social network analysis professor explained why this is the case. If a data model can only be drawn by crossing lines, then it is a non-planar graph.

It would be an understatement to say that this was enlightening to me. I was working at a customer site where we needed to untangle the interdependencies of all the applications that had grown over time through mergers and acquisitions, organic development, and external data providers.

Suddenly, I saw how these various systems were interconnected. It was a large-scale graph. The individual application data models were themselves data models. My memories of my high school experiences in mechanical drawing burst into my mind, and I saw that those were graphs, especially the parts where he was explaining the importance of showing how one line of a drawing was "in front of" or "behind" another line.

I remembered a documentary I had seen years before about Fractal[27] Geometry and Star Trek II. In Star Trek II, the scene where the Genesis planet was formed was the first computer-generated sequence entirely based on Fractal

---

[27] https://en.wikipedia.org/wiki/Fractal

Geometry. In the mid-1990s, I had a fractal generator on my computer. My kids used to play with it to see all the pretty pictures that the computer would generate. The image of the Genesis planet forming from the movie scene rampaged through my head.

I realized that a large-scale enterprise with many applications related to each other through data flows, with each application having its data model, is a fractal. One of the critical aspects of fractal geometry is self-similarity at scale. The overall data architecture where many applications are tied together is a graph. Within each application, the individual databases supporting such applications have their own data model, which is a graph.

In my Coursera class, we were using a tool called Gephi.[28] Gephi is a social network analysis tool that allows the analyst to load a spreadsheet of nodes and edges. It will then visualize the data and perform several graph-based calculations that delve into the heart of graph theory. I created some random names of application systems, wrote a little script to generate connections between these random names, and loaded the script into Gephi that evening.

This is what it rendered:

------

[28] https://gephi.org/

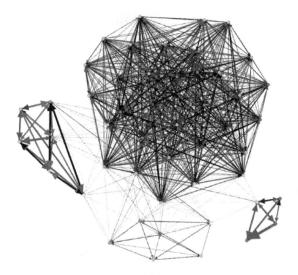

This was like the problem we were working on. If we could gather all the information about data transfers within the organization, we could quantify which systems had a more considerable impact on the entire ecosystem.

I did some further research on fractal geometry and found that you could, in fact, measure the fractal dimension of a graph.[29] My mind raced as I considered these things, so I had to walk around the building.

If an individual ERD (Entity Relationship Diagram) is a graph and an overall data architecture is a graph (although technically, it is more of a topology), we can measure each using both fractal geometry and standard traditional graph metrics.

[29] https://en.wikipedia.org/wiki/Fractal_dimension_on_networks

This simple understanding caused my mind to leap in so many different directions. I was amazed when I saw through the lens of mathematics the data modeling and data architecture work I had been doing for many years.

According to relational theory, the simple table that is part of a database is governed by rules. Now, it has become clear that the entire system is governed mathematically and can be measured quantitatively.

For several reasons, I could never actively apply these techniques to the problem at hand. This was likely because the lead on the project I was working on was using methods developed in the 1960s for analyzing the systems.

A few months later, I self-published my first book for Amazon Kindle, *Data Structure Graphs*. My mind was racing, full of possibilities, opportunities, and mathematical symbols swam before my eyes. I wrote and published the book to capture the essence of what I was experiencing and share this with the world. I have also presented some of these ideas at a few conferences.

Throughout the rest of this work, we will use graph metrics to understand our data structures better.

"In mathematics, a dense graph is a graph in which the number of edges is close to the maximal number of edges (where every pair of vertices is connected by one edge). The opposite, a graph with only a few edges, is a sparse graph. The distinction of what constitutes a dense or sparse graph is ill-defined and is often represented by 'roughly equal to' statements. Due to this, the way that density is defined often depends on the context of the problem."[30]

The proper definition of graph density here is how it relates to data structures. A data model that has a high graph density or is a highly dense graph is optimized for reading but not writing. A data model that has a low graph density or is a sparse graph is optimized for writing but not necessarily reading.

"In graph theory, eigenvector centrality (also called Eigencentrality or prestige score[1]) is a measure of the influence of a node in a connected network. Relative scores are assigned to all nodes in the network based on the concept that connections to high-scoring nodes contribute more to the score of the node in question than equal connections to low-scoring nodes. A high eigenvector score means that a node is connected to many nodes which themselves have high scores."[31]

---

[30] https://en.wikipedia.org/wiki/Dense_graph

[31] https://en.wikipedia.org/wiki/Eigenvector_centrality

Data Model

"If you took one-tenth the energy you put into complaining and applied it to solving the problem, you'd be surprised by how well things can work out... Complaining does not work as a strategy. We all have finite time and energy. Any time we spend whining is unlikely to help us achieve our goals. And it won't make us happier." - Randy Pausch

When the opportunity arises to build something new, there is an innate human tendency to begin building impulsively. The allure of immediate action often overshadows the seemingly tedious necessity of meticulously planning and designing the project. This oversight can lead to unforeseen challenges and potential pitfalls down the road.

The desire for instant results and the thrill of seeing one's vision come to life can sometimes overshadow the importance of laying a solid foundation. Focusing on instant results without considering long-term consequences is akin to setting off on a journey without a map, increasing the risk of getting lost or sidetracked. Careful planning will ensure that the project's outcome aligns with the desired result.

> *In many "Agile" projects that I have been involved in, engineers abdicate the design responsibilities to their users, thus throwing away years of experience and expertise for the sake of "getting something out the door quickly."*

Overlooking the design process can result in missed opportunities for innovation and optimization. During this phase, critical decisions are made regarding the product's functionality, aesthetics, and user experience. Neglecting this step can prevent the project from reaching its full potential, hindering the chance to innovate and optimize.

While the temptation to immediately start building is understandable, it's crucial to resist this urge and prioritize the design phase. This discipline and focus on thoughtful planning can help avoid potential pitfalls, optimize the project's outcome, and significantly increase the chances of success.

I learned this at an early age during the classes I took on mechanical drawing. Having all of the specifications clearly described, visualized, and drawn out may take a little time, but the advantages far outweigh the disadvantages. Rather than wasting weeks of programming time, a few hours of data model design work between a data architect and someone familiar with the business process can lay a foundation to speed up development work and ensure that performance and scalability are built in from the ground up.

When I talk about Data Structure Synthesis, the idea is to design Data Structures that exist within a Data Model and can serve the needs of more than a single use case. Well-thought-out Data Structures will continue to become more important because data will continue to grow.

Too often, I have been involved in projects where the team needed help with performance. When I looked at the data structures, I saw good portions of the problem. This data structure needs to be changed. These data types are wrong. This table has too many indexes. The data in these tables need to be separated for reporting.

The response to these recommendations has been, more often than not, "Nobody is asking for those changes."

Ignoring technical experts and having the only people who can drive changes within an organization be the users of the data systems, firmly puts an organization in the category of having the inmates run the asylum. To be clear, the voice of the customer is absolutely an essential input into the overall design and maintenance of a system. However, their voice should be tempered by experience, expertise, and explanation. The experience of the architects responsible for the system, combined with the expertise of the engineers putting the system together, along with clear explanations to the customers making requests what the impact of their requests will be on the system itself.

Every non-trivial word we use is burdened with meaning, interpretation, and context to be understood. Using visual data modeling tools like SqlDBM, Vertabelo, ERWin, and the like can relieve some of the confusion when designing a system.

> *Having clear images showing how one data*
> *structure relates to another data structure and*
> *demonstrating the overall flow of data from one*
> *structure to another through the lifecycle of the*
> *system allows architect, engineer, designer, user,*
> *and consumer, to understand how the data works.*

The application then becomes a shepherd, herding the data from one place to another, and the design of the user experience can be aligned with the overall goal of ensuring that the data the system is giving a voice to tell the story that everyone expects.

All these thoughts boil down to having a well-designed Data Model. The Data Model is an artifact to help communicate with the business, isolate performance issues, improve responsiveness, and drive the creation of new products.

The previous sections of this book were mostly about mathematical concepts; now, we can begin to discuss how to apply those concepts to designing a database with a data model.

A data model represents a schema within a database.

Schema

A schema is a logical collection of database objects that serve a common purpose. There are tables, views, and other objects the data architect has identified that belong within the schema to support the application, data mart, set of data products, integration layer, or presentation layer for visualizing the data from within the enterprise.

Now that we have identified the high-level objects within a relational database, let's show how they are all connected and used to support data querying and manipulation. Let's show two schemas in our database: OPERATIONS and FINANCE. Within each schema, there is a table named Supplier, along with some other tables that will be anonymous for the moment.

The operations team needs to know a supplier's name, reliability, schedule, available parts, raw materials, and who to contact to ensure on-time delivery of supplies.

Once the finance team purchases a part or some material, they need to know the supplier's banking information, any terms and conditions associated with the purchase, and who to contact to work out any payment arrangements.

The needs of each team within the organization are different. The data for each is considered production data, so it should not be stored in a separate database built within the enrichment platform. Logically separate according to the schema. When querying each of these tables, the whole structure of the query for them would be:

Select SomeColumn from database.schema.tablename

For operations:

```
Select SupplierName from ACTA_DB_PROD.OPERATIONS.Supplier
```

For finance:

```
Select SupplierName from ACTA_DB_PROD.FINANCE.Supplier
```

Each of these queries returns different results since they are storing other data.

Within your query tool of choice, once you create a connection with Snowflake, you will have a session to exchange information between your application and Snowflake. Each session will have a current database and schema in each of the examples above. As long as the user's session is connected to the correct database and schema, each query could look precisely the same.

For operations:

```
Select SupplierName from Supplier
```

For finance:

```
Select SupplierName from Supplier
```

Since each session connects to the same database but with different schemas, these two queries are equivalent to the queries listed above. They will each return different data.

One tool that can be invaluable in understanding how to use the tables identified in a schema and the relationships between the various tables is an Entity Relationship Diagram (ERD). The following is an example of an ERD from my book, *The Enrichment Game*.

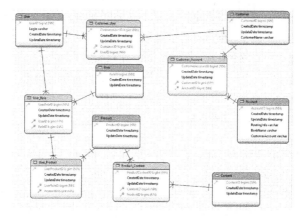

Here, you can see the names of the tables, which columns are keys, the data type of each column, all the available columns, and the relationship each table has with its partners. The tables representing many-to-many relationships appear in different colors.

Humans have evolved over millions of years to be exceptionally good at understanding visual phenomena quickly. Once you know the meaning of these "dots and lines" of an ERD, you can very easily create queries based on the structure of the schema. For example, if you want to find out the name of the bank a customer uses, you need to join the Customer, Customer_Account, and Account tables. Without this visual representation, it may take some data exploration to get to the correct query in this schema.

Design

Designing a database can feel like a religious or political battle. Opinions run deep when it comes to database design, and usually, the person or team most closely connected to the higher-ranking executive is allowed to create or approve the design of a database. I could tell horror stories about seeing databases built that I knew would fail to meet the requirements because someone thought they were the best designer for the job.

One of the worst "Agile" quotes I have ever heard in the realm of database design was from a team lead who approached a DBA on my team and said, "I need you to design these tables; they need to go into production this afternoon."

My first thought was that this was not agility—this was insanity.

Let's discuss database design at a very high level. Many other books can guide you on your journey to becoming a better database designer. After I have covered more mathematical topics, I will discuss database design again.

Except in this database design section, I will explain how to use all of the mathematical tools we have developed through the book to produce a robust, flexible, and, need I say, agile data model that will support an application, an enrichment platform, a visualization tool, and data science feature engineering.

Only under certain circumstances can you design a database entirely for yourself. Most of the time, the database design supports an application, an enrichment platform, or a visualization tool like a business intelligence server.

One of the critical things I learned early on when designing a database was that you must pay careful attention to the requirements. A good first step is to identify the nouns in the requirements. These will represent entities and verbs will represent relationships.

My high-school English teacher, who made us diagram sentences, finally pulled one on me.

Understanding earlier that we can interpret a table as a sentence was interesting. I found it amusing that designing databases effectively hinges on interpreting distinct parts of speech from a set of requirements.

I was sure the instructor had been an English professor in one of the classes I took on using ERWin as a data modeling tool. I did not start my formal writing journey until much later after this class, so I had not yet been introduced to *The Elements of Style* by Strunk and White.

The instructor repeated this quote from The Elements of Style when covering the section in ERWin where you document an attribute or an entity.

"Vigorous writing is concise. A sentence should contain no unnecessary words, a paragraph no unnecessary sentences, for the same reason that a drawing should have no unnecessary lines and a machine no unnecessary parts. This requires not that the writer make all sentences short or avoid all detail and treat subjects only in outline, but that every word tell."[32]

---

[32] https://en.wikipedia.org/wiki/The_Elements_of_Style

My high school English teacher and this instructor would have gotten along well. In addition to the names of entities, he showed us how to apply action phrases to our foreign key definitions. Entity A performs some action on Entity B.

By doing this in a well-thought-out manner, the data model diagram, or ERD as it is called, becomes not just an artifact produced as a side effect of the design process.

The data model represents a living document that can show pictorially not only the entities and relationships but also the actions to perform to relate one entity to another.

A well-crafted data model serves as the architect's blueprint, guiding the construction of a robust and scalable information system. To embark on this journey of data modeling, one must embrace these fundamental best practices that lay the groundwork for success:

- **Understand your business requirements**: Before diving into the intricacies of entities, attributes, and relationships, take the time to thoroughly understand the business requirements that your data model must fulfill. Engage with stakeholders, domain experts, and end-users to comprehensively understand the data they interact with, the processes they follow, and the insights they seek. This engagement with stakeholders should be a conversation. Many project managers work diligently to separate the people doing the work from the people requesting the work.

- **Separate the people wanting something from those doing the work**: At the architect level, the architect lays out a long-term design and data model. This data model will be used to meet many needs as time goes on. In today's world of throwing away people, the expertise needed to do this takes some time to learn. We must leverage the expertise of the data architect or data modeler.

- **Adopt a conceptual approach**: Begin your data modeling journey with a conceptual model that captures the high-level entities and their relationships, devoid of implementation details. This abstract representation provides a clear and concise overview of the data landscape, fostering a shared understanding among stakeholders. Having a graph structure with only entities as the dots and relationships as the lines for visualization purposes helps communicate the design to non-technical people.

- **Strive for simplicity and clarity**: Embrace the elegance of simplicity in your data model. Avoid unnecessary complexity and strive for clarity in naming conventions, relationships, and data types. A well-structured and intuitive model facilitates comprehension, maintenance, and future enhancements. Earlier, I showed how a table could represent a sentence—not a well-formed sentence, but a sentence, nonetheless.

In writing better descriptive information about the relationships, the data model can move from

A Student FK01 Class

To

A Student is in a Class

- **Normalize your data or do not**: It depends on what you are trying to accomplish. Normalization, the process of organizing data to minimize redundancy and dependency, is pivotal in ensuring data integrity and consistency. Adhering to normalization principles creates a model that is less prone to anomalies and easier to maintain. Normalizing data works well for an application, and from a graph perspective, the density of the graph is sparse. Data is organized, redundancy is minimized, and proper dependencies are captured at the application's data layer.

  Denormalizing data happens when we want to do other things. A data vault itself is a hybrid of normalization and denormalization. The density of a data vault becomes denser than that of a well-designed application. The bus architecture pioneered by Ralph Kimball will be much denser than the application or a set of data vault structures[33].

- **Choose the correct data types**: Selecting appropriate data types for your attributes is crucial for accurate representation and efficient storage.

---

[33] https://www.kimballgroup.com/data-warehouse-business-intelligence-resources/kimball-techniques/kimball-data-warehouse-bus-architecture/

Consider the nature of the data, its range of values, and the operations it will undergo to make informed choices. For cloud databases like Snowflake, the data type is less critical because of the elastic nature of the storage. For data systems where the database is managed by a group of database administrators or DataOps engineers, the storage requirements for a set of tables become very important.

When looking at large-scale systems, the location of the data types within a table can significantly impact the storage used. Having similar data types, regardless of what they represent, stored in the table adjacent to each other compared with having columns with dissimilar data types next to each other can affect storage.

I most recently tested this on the open-source Postgres database using a local disk. The delta between the storage used as the volume of data increased was in the gigabyte range.

Let me give a particular example:

```
guid,char(8),char(8),char(8),int,int,int,date,date,date,varchar(4096),varchar(4096),varchar(4096)
```

It will use less storage, especially as the table becomes very wide than the table organized like the following:

```
guid,char(8),int,date,varchar(4096),char(8),int,date,varchar(4096),cha
r(8),int,date,varchar(4096)
```

I encourage the sophisticated reader to perform some of their tests experimenting with this concept and share feedback.

- **Define clear relationships**: Establish unambiguous relationships between entities, specifying cardinality and optionality. This ensures data consistency and enables accurate querying and analysis. Describe what the relationship is doing. If there needs to be more than a single relationship between two entities because they represent different things, so be it.

Take the time to put together a good data model, and it will be used, enriched, enhanced, updated, and extended for many years.

Volumetrics

I struggled to find an analogy for this because it can be complicated. Most people have the experience of being a customer in a bar so I will elaborate using a generic example of a bar.

Imagine you manage a bar. You need to pre-purchase all the ingredients for the drinks. There are seven alcoholic drinks and five non-alcoholic drinks. These base drinks make the rest of the mixed drinks.

The vendors of each drink sell different bulk volumes. You must anticipate the amount of drinking in your bar for the next week.

How much total volume of all drinks will you need considering the types of mixed drinks and pure drinks you sell?

In an environment where you must set up a database with finite disks, the bar question is the question faced by the data architect when implementing a new database.

She needs to know how each table will grow. Suppose the database provides various types of indexes. In that case, she must ascertain the specific index type and comprehend the correlation between the index size and the table in question. Also, for large-scale performance reasons, she places the indexes on disks different from the actual data.

In a non-elastic world, she must estimate the disk size when building the server that will host the database. Next, let us assume an additional requirement is geographic replication. The size of the disks will need to be available in every location for geographic replication.

Indeed, given a set of assumptions, we can leverage mathematical tools to justify the capital expenditure of all that disk space!

It all starts with the data model.

Each attribute of an entity has a data type, and depending on the data type, it will have a length in bytes. Add the size together with each attribute for an entity, then multiply by the estimated number of rows of growth per day, along with an estimate of the size of all indexes per table.

Add all that up, then multiply by 365 for a single year.

This will give you an estimate of the total volume for a single database. Now multiply that by the number of geo-replicated sites. Once the data architect has that number, she must estimate the disk size necessary for backups. How often does she need to do full backups or incremental backups? Are the backups compressed? What are the regulatory (legal) requirements for keeping old data available? Is there a defined process to remove data from the primary location after migrating the data to an enrichment platform?

Is the enrichment platform well-defined, and can you use that data model to estimate its volume?

The data modeler or data architect must answer these questions, which need to be rolled into the storage budget. Similar estimates would be necessary to determine the size and subsequently calculate the cost of disk space for databases with cloud-based elastic storage.

When delving into the section on economics, I will explain the balance of resource utilization amongst all infrastructure resources.

This section on volumetrics covers estimating the overall disk size. It does not cover thoughts associated with placing high-use tables on separate disks from low-use tables or distributing high-use tables amongst different disks.

The mathematical expression for calculating the disk volume of your data space follows. This is how to get the fundamental numbers that can be experimented with to give volume estimates for a single database.

Operations

DataOps is the current nom de guerre of the team that is responsible for:

- Keeping all the systems in the data ecosystem up and available.

- Ensuring all the data ecosystem is current with deployments of software releases both internal and external.

- Enforcing the governance, security, and change control rules.

- Guarding the stability of the data ecosystem.

- Creating, managing, moving, and removing non-production environments.

- Monitoring the performance of the production data ecosystem.

- Validating that the data gathered in an enrichment platform or made available for visualization purposes is the correct data and is fit for purpose.

- Data is moved, transformed, or archived in the most efficient manner to maintain high performance and data availability.

The data ecosystem consists of not only the database, but all the tools associated with data management. Although some of these tools may be custom-built, most are bought and adapted to the environment. Some examples of the types of tools within this ecosystem address data monitoring, data integration, data processing and analysis, data governance and management, and data security tools.

The skills required to do these things are wide-ranging, including system administration, scripting, knowledge of physical devices, and a decent amount of networking, to name a few. Data Operations personnel are not software developers.

Software developers are the customers of the data operations team. The other customers of the data operations team are finance executives, business analysts, research teams, data science teams, external suppliers, external vendors, partners, and anyone who needs access to the data that runs the enterprise.

When it comes to the care, feeding, and safety of the enterprise's data, the data operations team is the most critical team asset in an organization.

Category Theory

"*A powerful aspect of abstraction is that many different situations become the same when you forget some details.*" - Eugenia Cheng

In my broad survey of advanced mathematics to see what other things I had worked with that had a proper mathematical name, I stumbled across category theory by listening to a TED talk by Eugenia Cheng. By the way, she is a fantastic author. I have read most of her books.

I will give a precise definition of category theory shortly. It explains *how to transform one mathematical object into another,* so I am including it here.

I wrote the previous statement as if it were profound. I will bet you may think, "What is the significance?"

Many books about databases cover design, implementation, performance, and operations. Only those covering data integration cover how to transform data structures (tables) from one structure to another. Even then, most books like that are vendor-focused and want to explain how their tool is the best thing in the world for data transformations.

In the next section, I will cover ETL or ELT processes. That section covers the how, and this section covers the why.

In a previous section, we covered how a table can be considered a mathematical object. A table is an implementation of a relation, and each row is an implementation of a RelVar. We are creating a set of sets that contains the data.

Category theory explains the mathematical process of transforming one mathematical object into another.

Data models for applications, integration, reporting, and analytics all serve different needs of the enterprise. These other needs require different structures. When you only look at the structures in isolation, it will not be obvious why we need these structures.

We can easily demonstrate that different data structures for the same data can have very different volume footprints.

I have repeatedly heard it said that storage is cheap. It can be if we appropriately govern the use of storage. If unmanaged, storage can quickly get out of control. Only someone who looks across all the enterprise's needs will see when storage is out of control in one place or another.

When we cover information theory and column entropy, I will demonstrate how structure can affect volume.

The least well-governed set of data structures is the application database. Application databases are optimized for application performance. They may only follow best practices associated with application management rather than best practices related to data.

Indexes can improve the performance of select queries in non-snowflake databases. However, a liberal use of indexes can degrade performance, depending on the database's physical layout, memory, and other factors.

Indexes are lightweight compared to the tables they index. However, in the world of database performance, every action has consequences.

A table with one index requires at least two Input and Output (IO) operations. As a reminder, the fastest code is the code that never executes. The same table with two indexes requires at least three IO operations. The number of I/O operations for a table is always (number of indexes) +1 for write operations. The index may reduce the number of IO operations needed for read operations if built and used correctly.

Once again, I ask the question: why transform data structures?

An application has requirements for data capture and performance. Reporting or analytics data products have different requirements for reading data and performance. Having scheduled processes that copy data from the application to an enrichment platform and then remove that data from the application will improve the application's performance and give a set of data structures that can be tuned differently for back-end internal use cases.

Now, let us move on to the more precise definition of category theory and show the mechanics of transforming data mathematically.

Category theory is a branch of mathematics that provides a powerful and abstract way to study mathematical structures and their relationships. It is a bit like "meta-mathematics" that does not focus on specific mathematical objects (like numbers or shapes) but on the patterns and connections between them. Here are the fundamental concepts of category theory:

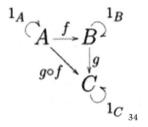

- **Objects:** In category theory, we start with the concept of an "object." An object can be anything: a number, *a set*, a group, a topological space, or even something more abstract, like the concept of time. Objects are like the building blocks of our mathematical universe. In the illustration, the capital letters A, B, and C are the objects.

- **Arrows:** The heart of category theory lies in studying how objects are connected or related to each other. We represent these connections by "arrows" or "morphisms." Think of morphisms as

---

[34] https://commons.wikimedia.org/wiki/File:Category_SVG.svg

processes, functions, transformations, or any way you can go from one object to another. In the illustration, the morphisms are f, g, and $g \circ f$. The loops are identity arrows.

- **Composition**: You can combine arrows through a process called "composition." If you have an arrow from object A to object B and another from B to C, you can "compose" them to get an arrow from A to C. This composition operation is associative, which means the order you compose them does not matter. In our image above, the $g \circ f$ function shows that if you perform the function f on A, followed by g, the result will be C.

- **Identity Arrows**: For each object, an "identity arrow" represents doing nothing. Think of it as a function that takes an object and returns the same object. This identity arrow is a fundamental concept in category theory. In the illustration, 1_a, 1_b, and 1_c are the identity arrows.

- **Categories**: A category is a collection of objects and arrows that obey specific rules:

  - Every object has an identity arrow.

  - Arrow composition is associative.

  - Arrows behave well with identities when composed.

- **Abstraction**: This is the beauty of category theory. Category theory allows mathematicians to abstract away the specific details of mathematical structures and focus on the common patterns and relationships shared by various mathematical domains. It helps identify similarities between seemingly different areas of mathematics.

- **Universal properties**: Category theory introduces the concept of "universal properties" to describe fundamental relationships between objects in a category. These properties help mathematicians understand the essence of different mathematical structures.

- **Functors and natural transformations**: In category theory, concepts like "functors" and "natural transformations" describe how categories relate to each other. *Functors* are like mathematical transformations between categories, and natural transformations provide a way to compare different functors.

- **Applications**: Category theory is not just for pure mathematics. It has applications in computer science (especially in programming language theory and type theory), physics (e.g., quantum mechanics and relativity), and even philosophy (e.g., in the study of metaphysics and the nature of mathematical objects).

Okay, the math lesson is over. How many of you have been working on an overall design where you draw letters, arrows, boxes, lines, and circles on a whiteboard? Most often, these are design sessions for migrating data from one area to another.

Guess what?

You were doing category theory.

The source mathematical object is a set (relation/RelVar/table).

The target mathematical object is also a set (relation/RelVar/table).

The morphism is the transformation code.

Congratulations, you have been a mathematician for as long as you have been a data architect!

In later sections, I am going to add a layer of abstraction. There are specific table structures that (with some fuzzy glasses) could be interpreted as mathematical objects separate from the relations we were discussing previously.

ETL and ELT

"The final step of the ETL process is the physical structuring and loading of data into the presentation area's target dimensional models. Because the primary mission of the ETL system is to hand off the dimension and fact tables in the delivery step, these subsystems are critical. Many of these defined subsystems focus on dimension table processing, such as surrogate key assignments, code lookups to provide appropriate descriptions, splitting, or combining columns to present the appropriate data values, or joining underlying third normal form table structures into flattened denormalized dimensions. In contrast, fact tables are typically large and time consuming to load, but preparing them for the presentation area is typically straightforward. When the dimension and fact tables in a dimensional model have been updated, indexed, supplied with appropriate aggregates, and further quality assured, the business community is notified that the new data has been published." - Ralph Kimball

The ETL process stands for Extract, Transform, and Load. It is a data integration process used in data warehousing and analytics to extract data from multiple sources, transform it into a consistent format, and load it into a target location, typically a data warehouse.

The ETL process is needed because businesses today deal with vast amounts of data from various sources, such as databases, spreadsheets, and external systems. However, this data is often disparate and needs to be formatted in a way suitable for analysis or reporting. The ETL process helps address this challenge by enabling organizations to extract data from different sources, transform it into a consistent and usable format, and load it into a centralized location for analysis.

The ETL process typically involves the following steps:

- **Extraction:** Data is extracted from various sources, such as databases, spreadsheets, APIs, or log files.

- **Transformation:** The extracted data is then transformed or cleansed to ensure consistency, quality, and accuracy. This may involve activities such as data cleaning, data validation, data enrichment, aggregations, and conversions.

- **Loading:** The transformed data is loaded into a target location, often a data warehouse or a data mart, where it can be stored, organized, and accessed for analysis and reporting.

To extract data effectively from the database that supports an application, one must identify the data in the application that has been created or modified.

The process for this is called Change Data Capture (CDC). CDC encapsulates all the various techniques for capturing the changed data.

A well-designed application database will naturally store metadata columns that specify a timestamp for when a record is created and when it is modified. Tools are also available to identify the changed data. Remember the section on the data ecosystem? This is one of the various tools the data operations team is responsible for.

The ETL process is crucial for organizations because it helps them consolidate and integrate data from disparate sources, enabling unified reporting, analysis, and decision-making. It provides a structured and organized view of the data, making it easier to understand patterns, trends, and insights.

On the other hand, ELT, which stands for Extract, Load, Transform, is a variation of the traditional ETL process. In ELT, the data is first extracted and loaded into the target location, typically a data lake or a data warehouse, without any transformation. The transformation step is then performed within the target location using specialized tools or technologies. This approach leverages the processing power and scalability of the target system to perform complex transformations on the data.

The critical difference between ETL and ELT is the timing and location of the transformation step. In ETL, the data is transformed before loading it into the target system, while in ELT, the data is loaded first, and the transformation is performed within the target system. ELT can be advantageous when dealing with large volumes of data or complex transformations, as it allows for parallel processing and scalability.

A specific responsibility of the data ops team is monitoring the processes that move data, which are called pipelines. This copying "movement" of data from one place to another is only one of the many processes that data ops are responsible for from the perspective of continuous improvement.

One of the better process improvement frameworks is Six Sigma. A few essential aspects of Six Sigma that are important for DataOps are:

- A clear focus on achieving measurable and quantifiable financial returns from any Six Sigma project.

- An increased emphasis on strong and enthusiastic management leadership and support.

- A clear commitment to making decisions based on verifiable data and statistical methods rather than assumptions and guesswork.[35]

---

[35] https://www.nvtquality.com/white-papers/introduction-to-six-sigma-methodology/

- Continuous efforts to achieve stable and predictable process results.

- Achieving sustained quality improvement requires commitment from the entire organization, particularly from top-level management.

To best accomplish this goal of increased stability and reduced variation, every process that copies, moves, modifies, updates, or transforms data in the production environment must provide at least timestamp information about itself.

The data must then be collected and consolidated for statistical analysis, which is one of the DataOps team's most important responsibilities.

The enterprise's decision-makers need to be confident that the data they are working with is current, valid, and appropriate for decision-making.

Metric Spaces

"Topology is the science of fundamental pattern and structural relationships of event constellations." - R. Buckminster Fuller

One key difference between a normal graph and a topology is the distance between the points. In a graph, the distance between two points is undefined; it is only defined that they are connected.

"A metric space is a set together with a notion of distance between its elements, usually called points."[36]

By defining the data flows between two systems as having a metric of one and taking a more extensive look at the enterprise's ecosystem to understand all the data flowing between any two systems, you have a data structure topology.

---

[36] https://en.wikipedia.org/wiki/Metric_space

Topology is a branch of mathematics that deals with the properties and characteristics of spaces, particularly connectedness and continuity. It explores the fundamental concepts of continuity, proximity, and relationships within a given space.

When it comes to networks and data flow diagrams, topology plays a crucial role in analyzing and understanding their structure and behavior. In computer networks, topology refers to the physical or logical arrangement of devices and connections that form a network. It describes how devices are interconnected and how data flows through the network. The data structure topology would be virtual rather than physical because there may be clusters of servers that represent a single source or destination. When it comes to data flow diagrams, topology helps visualize and understand the flow of data within a system or process. Data flow diagrams represent the movement of data from one component to another, highlighting the interactions and transformations that take place at each step.

I have not applied topology to the study of enterprise data architecture. In my attempts at synthesizing the world of data architecture and mathematics in more detail, many people use the term topology only to refer to the network within an organization. I am treating the network topology as only a single layer of the topology of the enterprise, and layering on top of that a data structure topology that includes any mechanism to exchange data between two systems would give the data architects of the world a new perspective on how to represent the large scale systems that we build.

Data Vault

"The data vault is the optimal choice for modeling the EDW in the DW 2.0 framework." - Bill Inmon

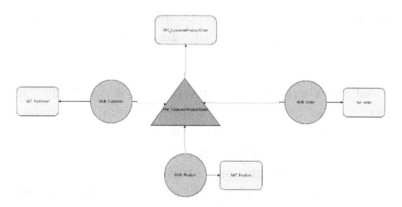

Dan Linstedt invented the data vault methodology in the late 1990s . He designed this approach to respond to the challenges faced by traditional data warehousing methods in accommodating changing business requirements and maintaining data traceability. The data vault architecture, including the concept of hubs, was developed to provide a scalable, agile, and auditable solution for data integration and analytics.

I am not an authorized trainer for the data vault; I am only certified with the methodology. I encourage the astute reader interested in learning more about data vault to either liberally search for Data Vault Alliance information or reach out to me, and I will point you in the right direction. Also, a great book to get guidance on implementing the data vault is "The Elephant in the Fridge" by John Giles.

My first exposure to data vault was when I met Dan Linstedt as part of a project we were implementing while I was the data operations manager of a finance company. One of my interactions with Dan appears in the introduction of this book. This would have been in 2005 or 2006. I learned the approach quickly, which worked fine for the small level of integration needed in our project. As I changed companies, I began to look for ways to implement the data vault.

I did a few experimental projects with it, and finally, in 2007, I had my first large-scale integration project that required a data vault approach. I had limited resources, and my team was constantly being called away to support other projects. As I became more frustrated with the lack of progress, I began looking at the patterns. Three main data structures need to be implemented.

For those data structures, I could create base templates and reuse those templates as load procedures.

That solved one problem.

Next, I needed information on what data was copied from which source system and table. During the business analysis portion of my work, I created a source-to-target map document that showed how all the tables related.

At the time, I was still using PERL from my days building back-end support systems for website startups. I created some templates and read the source to target maps. Then, I wrote out the templates as actual Pentaho ETL jobs. I imported the Pentaho jobs into the Pentaho UI. I did a few finishing touches, and over 100 Pentaho jobs were ready to run.

In one day of scripting!

Let me put that accomplishment in today's terminology. I created a metadata-driven automation process for creating ETL jobs to populate hubs, links, and satellites in under a single day (in early 2008). This allowed me to start populating the data vault I had designed so we could begin testing it.

Dan Linstedt came to New York, where I was working on this project. He reviewed my progress, and from a technical perspective, things were looking good.

It is always the things you do not know that will negatively impact your life—something neither of us could have predicted would happen soon after that.

"March 17, 2008: Bear Stearns, with $46 billion of mortgage assets that had not been written down and $10 trillion in total assets, faced bankruptcy; instead, in its first emergency meeting in 30 years, the Federal Reserve agreed to guarantee its bad loans to facilitate its acquisition by

JPMorgan Chase for $2/share. A week earlier, the stock was trading at $60/share; a year earlier, it traded for $178/share. The buyout price was increased to $10/share the following week."[37]

This was not the beginning of the 2008 financial crisis. That had been brewing for some time. The company I worked for was a startup with close ties to Wall Street. As the crisis started to unfold, they, along with many others, began large-scale layoffs.

Many books cover the 2008 Financial crisis, so I will not offer any opinions about its cause or overall impact. What I do know is the crisis did throw my career into a tailspin for a few years. I could not focus on building data vault environments for some time. I focused on overall data operations management as I worked to stay employed until the economy settled down.

My conversations with Dan during those projects inspired me. I kept working on applying ways to do metadata-driven automation, identify business keys, and load data correctly and efficiently with full auditability.

Later, as I began my trek to become a data scientist, I revisited these problems from the perspective of the techniques I was learning. This book is an artifact of that research, which started in a hot upstairs cubicle of a warehouse in Queens in 2007.

---

[37] https://en.wikipedia.org/wiki/2007%E2%80%932008_financial_crisis

Hub

A HUB in a data vault database is *a unique list* of business keys representing a particular business entity, such as a customer or product. These hubs act as central points for connecting different data entities within the data warehouse.

"A unique list"? Oh, yes, a set.

Excluding the appropriate metadata columns required by the methodology, a hub is a set of business keys.

Suddenly, we are back to the beginning of the book, where I introduced set theory.

In mathematical notation, you could look at a hub as this:

$\{H_c\}$ Where subscript c represents the customer.

Suddenly, what was once data modeling begins to look more like mathematics.

Referring to our examples in category theory and the terminology of the ETL/ELT process, the T (Transformation) of the data from one data structure to the other is a forgetful functor[38].

The forgetful functor strips the structure or properties from the input object before mapping it to the output object. For a hub, the source of the data is, of course, a table

---

[38] https://en.wikipedia.org/wiki/Forgetful_functor

containing the business key and other attributes related to the business key and the primary key. To populate a HUB, using a higher level of abstraction and ignoring things like surrogate keys and metadata, the input is a relation, and the output is a set.

Probability

"Probability theory is nothing but common sense reduced to calculation." - Pierre-Simon Laplace

Probability is a branch of mathematics that deals with uncertainty and randomness. It provides a framework for quantifying and understanding uncertain events. At its core, probability is concerned with predicting the likelihood of different outcomes in each situation.

Terms within probability include:

- **Sample space (Ω)**: The sample space, often denoted as Ω, is the set of all possible outcomes of a random experiment. For example, if you roll a standard six-sided die, the sample space is {1, 2, 3, 4, 5, 6}. It encompasses all the possible results of the experiment.

- **Event**: An event is a subset of the sample space, representing one or more specific outcomes of the random experiment. We denote events with capital letters (e.g., A, B, C). For example, if you are interested in the event of rolling an even number on a six-sided die, it would be represented as A = {2, 4, 6}.

- **Probability function (P):** The probability function, often denoted as P, assigns a numerical value between 0 and 1 to each event. It quantifies the likelihood of an event occurring. The probability of an event A is written as P(A).

- **Probability space:** A probability space is a mathematical structure that consists of three elements:

  - Sample space (Ω): The set of all possible outcomes of a random experiment.

  - Event space (F): A collection of subsets of the sample space Ω, where each subset represents an event.

  - Probability measure (P): A function that assigns probabilities to events in the event space, satisfying the probability axioms.

Using the analogy above of the six-sided die, let us populate a hub we will call HUB_Die $\{H_d\}$

What is the content of the HUB_Die?

$$\{1, 2, 3, 4, 5, 6\}$$

So, for any event roll of the die, one of these six numbers is the expected outcome. Hence, the probability of any one number coming up on top is $\frac{1}{6}$ correct?

Put on those fuzzy glasses now.

For a HUB_Product $\{H_p\}$, what is the probability that a customer will purchase any given product?

$$\frac{1}{|H_p|}$$

Let me elaborate a bit on this notation since I brought something new into the denominator.

The cardinality of a set is the size of the set.[39] We denote this by the vertical bars on either side of the name of the set. For the set H_p the cardinality of the set is $|H_p|$ or how many rows are in the HUB_Product table.

This is a mathematical definition. A correctly populated hub can perform probability calculations without further transformations.

Luckily, according to the data vault standards, the hub does not exist in isolation. There may be one or more satellites related to the hub, and there could be one or more links related to the hub. As mentioned previously, the satellite contains contextual information related to the hub. By using a satellite to filter the number of records in the hub to do probability calculations, the astute data scientist could perform some interesting probability studies using only a hub and a satellite.

---

[39] https://en.wikipedia.org/wiki/Cardinality

Link

A data vault link is a structural element used to connect two or more data vault hubs or satellites.

Data vault links serve several vital purposes within the methodology:

- **Capturing relationships**: Links represent relationships between hubs. They help maintain the integrity and context of these relationships within the data warehouse.

- **Handling many-to-many relationships**: Data vault excels at modeling many-to-many relationships, which are common in complex business environments. Links enable the modeling of these relationships efficiently.

- **Flexibility and scalability**: Links provide flexibility in handling changes in business requirements and data sources. When new relationships emerge or existing ones change, data vault links can adapt without significant structural alterations.

- **Supporting historical data**: Just like hubs and satellites, links can have associated historical data, allowing the tracking of changes in relationships over time. This historical context is crucial for auditing, compliance, and analysis.

- **Simplifying data integration**: Links streamline the process of integrating data from different sources by establishing a standardized way to represent relationships. This reduces complexity in ETL (Extract, Transform, Load) processes.

There are a few ways of interpreting a link's function and what it could represent mathematically. We have already touched on graph theory. One thing that the link can describe is the relationship between two or more hubs. Before drawing your attention to the following image, I need to elaborate on the metadata attributes of every fundamental structure in a data vault.

Each table type has several metadata columns. The most important one for our discussion purposes is the LDTS (Load Date Time Stamp), which is the timestamp for when the data is loaded into the data vault structures.

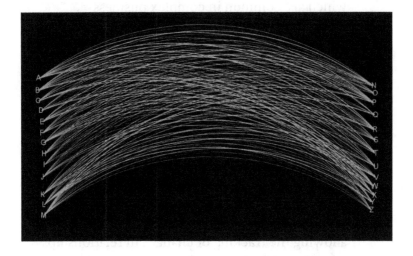

Think of every link in a data vault structure as an n-partite graph where n is the number of hubs that are related together in that link. In the above example, Hub 1 has the values of A through M as the business keys, and Hub 2 has the values N through Z. Since there are only two hubs related to this link, we have a bipartite graph in this image.

Depending on the number of hubs that are related via a link, the type of graph to represent will always be an n-partite graph.

Calculus

"One of the pleasures of looking at the world through mathematical eyes is that you can see certain patterns that would otherwise be hidden." - Steven Strogatz

Calculus is a branch of mathematics that deals with the study of change. It provides a robust framework for understanding how quantities vary and how they relate to each other.

Everyone faces their challenges in life. One of my biggest challenges, but also my greatest joy, is expressed in my youngest daughter's life. Makenzi had been designated "special needs" and given the label of "Autistic" when she was young. She is a joy to be around on her good days but a nightmare on her bad days. We always suspected that there was something more to what was going on with her than just the label of Autistic. You see, the challenges we faced with her as a family forced me to be not only the primary breadwinner but the only breadwinner.

It was not until she was twenty-two that we were able to get a proper diagnosis of San Filippo Syndrome, or

Mucopolysaccharidosis III.[40] When we finally got the diagnosis, we were at first pleased because this explained so many of her symptoms, behaviors, and eccentricities. We were able to find a community that had been through some of our struggles and found other people who understood what we had been dealing with. Of course, with the good news also comes the bad.

It is **terminal**, with no known cure.

Your daughter is going to die, and there is nothing you can do about it!

Due to this challenge, my mathematical education could have been more active, and I could only study things when the opportunity arose. Taking formal classes had always been out of the question because her presentation of various symptoms was incredibly unpredictable.

While this could be a challenge, I was able to turn this into something of an opportunity because I continued to work as a database administrator, data architect, and ultimately a data scientist through time as this horrible disease stripped her of every natural capability that has evolved in humans through time.

Why do I mention my daughter's story in the middle of this book about discovering applicable mathematics concepts to data architecture?

I have read stories of scientific and mathematical breakthroughs throughout history. Quite a few of them are

---

[40] https://en.wikipedia.org/wiki/Mucopolysaccharidosis

serendipitous. Some of them are trying through hard work, trying to crack a problem. There are enough stories of someone working hard to understand something, then going on vacation, taking a break, or engaging in other activities and having a monstrous epiphany to reinforce the concept of the magnificent multilayered evolved calculating machine known as the human brain.

I think of ideas that pop fully formed into my consciousness as having been running as a background process. These are not supernatural manifestations; they are just the consequences of natural human evolution, where our brains work on different things at different times.

Having to study mathematical concepts in one domain while working on practical applications of data structures and problem-solving in another domain occasionally brings two things together. Understanding the relationship between a link and calculus was one such experience.

In calculus, the concept of a derivative is used to understand the rates of change of something.

The derivative of a function represents its rate of change at a particular point. For the equation "$y = f(x)$," the derivative is denoted as F (x) or dy/dx. Some textbooks also use Greek symbols to illustrate this better.

$$\frac{\Delta y}{\Delta x}$$

Where Δy is the difference in the y values corresponding to the difference in the x values expressed as Δx. The formal definition is: $\frac{dy}{dx} = \lim_{\Delta \to 0} \frac{\Delta y}{\Delta x}$ I will gloss over the concept of limits for the moment to elaborate on this definition.

Suppose the derivative of the function $y = f(x)$ is $\frac{dy}{dx}$

The definition of the derivative is $\frac{dy}{dx} = \lim_{\Delta \to 0} \frac{\Delta y}{\Delta x}$ which is comparing the rate of change of one quantity with the rate of change of another as the rate of change goes to zero.

In that case, comparing the rates of change of two quantities as the limit of the rate of change of one of them goes to zero means that you are looking at the derivative of a *function!*

Therefore, a link could be considered a function.

This is one of the reasons I mentioned my daughter and the constant distractions she has provided for my education. As I was studying these mathematical concepts, I was unable to "start from the beginning, proceed through logically step by step until done." I could be working on studying a mathematical textbook one day and subsequently spending time with her in the hospital. Normal people would call this distracting and be unable to accomplish much during this time.

I am not normal.

What I had thought was one of my most significant weaknesses, in a moment of enlightenment, became one of my biggest strengths. I did not need to focus on these problems constantly. I could concentrate, disconnect to care for my girl, and then come back with some new insights.

Let us put this in data structure terminology. Given HUB_Y and HUB_X, which represent some business entities, the LINK_YX could represent the function $y = f(x)$. However, looking at the data in the link, this is not an obvious observation.

I stumbled upon something that specifically represented the derivative while working on volumetric estimations.

Running this query will give some numbers to work with:

```
SELECT YEAR(LDTS) || MONTH(LDTS) || DAY(LDTS) || HOUR(LDTS)
|| MINUTE(LDTS) as "DATETOMINUTE",count(Y_HK),count(X_HK)
  group by 1
  order by 1;
```

Depending on the load frequency of the link table will determine the granularity of time that you want to look at. Taking this data and subtracting the counts of row N+1 against row N, you get the delta that has been loaded.

Doing a visualization of this delta data will give you the values $\Delta Y_{\square}$, and $\Delta X_{\square}$. Working backward from this differential data, it is theoretically possible to identify the mathematical relationship between these two business keys.

In other words, with some creative application of calculus, you will be able to identify the actual function that $f(x, y, z, blah, ...)$ has been performed.

This alone is quite impressive.

One of the goals of most data science projects is to identify a mathematical equation that shows how two things are related. Feature engineering, regressions, and various machine-learning models are all employed to determine this relationship. In a data vault, this capability is built into the structure of how the data is represented.

The procedure for links relating more than two hubs is similar, but the math is different. You can expand this procedure to look at partial differential equations in multiple dimensions by looking at the various differentials. The YouTube video in the footnote shows some exciting use cases of PDEs in the analysis of fluid flow.

The expression you end up with when performing the differential analysis of a link with three business keys looks something like this:

$$\partial_x/\partial_t + \partial_y/\partial_t + \partial_z/\partial_t$$

As I mentioned in the section on the beginning of set theory, calculus works with infinitely small numbers when looking at the differentials. For our use cases, the infinitely small becomes less small. The volume of the metric we are looking at is at the exact grain of the query you are running to identify the time differentials. If you look at things second by second, the ∂_t is 1 second. As this changes, the ∂_t can become one minute, one hour, or one day.

Now that we have abstracted the data structures into mathematical functions, we should review a few more mathematical terms.

Derivatives play a crucial role in understanding how quantities change with respect to each other. We often express this relationship through differential equations, which are equations involving derivatives. We can classify these equations into two main types: ordinary differential equations (ODEs) and partial differential equations (PDEs).

ODEs involve derivatives of a single variable and are used to model dynamic processes where a single independent variable changes continuously. The most basic form of an ODE is the first-order ODE:

$$dy/dx = f(x, y)$$

Here, y represents the dependent variable, x is the independent variable, and f(x, y) is a function that defines y's rate of change with respect to x. ODEs can also be of higher order, involving higher-order derivatives.

ODEs have widespread applications in various fields, including physics, engineering, biology, and economics. For example, Newton's second law of motion, which relates force, mass, and acceleration, is a second-order ODE. In economics, ODEs can model economic growth and decay, while in biology, they can describe population dynamics.

Solving ODEs typically involves finding a function y(x) that satisfies the given equation and initial or boundary conditions. Depending on the complexity of the equation, this process can be analytical or numerical.

PDEs involve derivatives of multiple variables and describe systems where quantities depend on more than one independent variable and change with respect to space and time. The general form of a first-order PDE is:

$$\partial u/\partial t = F(x, y, z, t, \partial u/\partial x, \partial u/\partial y, \partial u/\partial z)$$

In this equation, u represents the dependent variable, t is time, (x, y, z) represent spatial coordinates (in our case, differentials between the number of records loaded at a given point in time, and F is a function that describes the rate of change of u with respect to both time and spatial coordinates, as well as the spatial derivatives ($\partial u/\partial x$, $\partial u/\partial y$, $\partial u/\partial z$).

PDEs are fundamental in describing a wide range of physics phenomena, such as heat conduction, fluid flow, and quantum mechanics. They are also essential in engineering for modeling complex systems like heat exchangers, electromagnetic fields, and structural vibrations.

Solving PDEs is challenging and depends on the specific problem and boundary conditions. Techniques for solving PDEs include variable separation, Fourier transforms, and numerical methods like finite differences and finite element analysis.

In the context of ordinary differential equations (ODEs) and partial differential equations (PDEs), derivatives are used to model and understand the dynamic behavior of systems involving one or multiple variables. ODEs describe the rate of change of a single variable with respect to an independent variable, while PDEs describe how a variable changes with respect to time and multiple spatial coordinates.

The power of derivatives lies in their ability to express complex relationships in a concise mathematical form, enabling scientists and engineers to solve real-world problems, optimize processes, and gain insights into the behavior of physical systems. Whether it is describing the motion of objects, modeling population growth, simulating heat conduction, or solving quantum mechanical problems, calculus and derivatives are indispensable tools for understanding the fundamental nature of change in the universe.

In the section on hubs, I showed a different notation for a hub based on the definition of a set. Now that I have explained that a link can be a function, let us combine them:

$$\{H_x\} \searrow \qquad \swarrow \{H_y\}$$

$$f(x, y)$$

Satellite

A data vault satellite is a critical component that plays a specific role in managing and enhancing the information stored within a data vault.

A data vault satellite is a supplementary structure within the data vault architecture that stores additional attributes and context for the data in the data vault's core structures, which are the hubs, links, and satellites. While hubs and links store the core business keys and relationships between data entities, satellites provide a place to store descriptive and contextual information, historical data, and metadata about the core data. The data vault satellite serves several important purposes:

- **Historical tracking**: Satellites preserve historical data. By storing different versions of attributes over time, they enable time-based analysis and reporting, which is crucial for understanding data changes and trends.

- **Descriptive information**: Satellites contain additional attributes that provide context and meaning to the core data. This can include textual descriptions, classifications, or any other relevant information that helps users interpret the data.

- **Metadata**: Satellites can store metadata such as data source information, data quality metrics, timestamps, and data lineage details, which are essential for data governance and lineage tracking.

Since a satellite contains primarily descriptive information, it is the closest of all three structures to being the relation we saw described before. Adding to our mathematical representation of data vault structures and the predicate nature of the satellite, the following could be a representation of a data vault using only mathematical symbols:

$$P_x(c_1, \ldots c_n) \rightarrow H_x \searrow \qquad \nearrow H_y \leftarrow P_y(c_{1,,}, c_n)$$

$$f(x, y)$$

Information theory/entropy

"Information is the resolution of uncertainty." - Claude Shannon

Information theory is a branch of mathematics and computer science that deals with quantifying and transmitting information. Claude Shannon developed it in the mid-20th century and has since found applications in various fields, including machine learning and artificial intelligence.

The fundamental concept that measures the uncertainty or randomness associated with a set of data is called entropy. The entropy of a discrete random variable X with a probability distribution of $P(x)$ is:

$$H(X) = -\sum_x P(x) \log_2(P(x))$$

X represents all outcomes of the random variable and $P(x)$ is the probability of each outcome. The higher the entropy, the more uncertain or random the data is and the more information it carries.

This fundamental concept of entropy is at the level of storage or transmission. This measurement of entropy is based on the bit, and because of Doctor Claude Shannon's work, we now have things like high-speed communication signals, fast computers, cloud-based storage environments, and the luxuries of the 21st century.

I explored information theory, hoping to find that someone else had solved one of the problems I struggled with in database design. The motivation for solving this problem evolved from my conversation with Dan Linstedt (again).

The question was: "How do we mechanically identify a business key[41] from a source system?"

Because a business key is not necessarily a technical database primary key, it can be challenging to identify without specific domain knowledge of the application.

As I explored information theory, it seemed to me it needed more at this higher level of abstraction. Information theory gives us the fundamental low-level techniques to manage the storage and transmission of data. It also allows us to verify that data is accurate between sender and receiver and from when the data was initially stored until it is used.

At the abstract level of a relation and implemented RelVar, it is a scalpel when a steak knife is needed. As I mentioned before, I will spare the reader from the various dead ends I reached. Instead, I will show you the solution:

Column entropy:

$$\Delta C_n^t \Big/ \Delta R_t$$

In words, this expression means:

---

[41] https://en.wikipedia.org/wiki/Natural_key

"For any column n with several rows R for a given period t, what is the unique rate of change of the individual column divided by the rate of change of the unique rows in this relation?"

This calculation gives us a metric for calculating the rate of change of a given column as compared to the rate of change of the entire relation for some time. The time-period could be a set of 500 records, all records for a day, or all records for an hour. This time-period is variable depending on the needs of the table's use case within the application.

The process for using this expression is:

1. Collect this information for various periods.

2. Use some standard statistical tools, such as the mean and variance of the resulting sets of numbers for each column.

3. Run a clustering algorithm against this data.

What will come out of the clustering algorithm is that some columns have a "similar" rate of change to others. These columns "belong together" in a database table. These columns are the predicates that change with the same frequency level, implying that they are descriptive predicates for the same key, whether defined or not. I had hoped that the output of this algorithm would be a smoking gun pointing to the business key of any table in a source system that was designed following application needs rather than best practices.

What it gave me was something far more general purpose than what I had set out to find.

This analysis technique definitively shows which columns should be grouped in one table based on rates of change. It may provide two groups, or it could give many more.

I have identified a few use cases for this technique, which I will explain shortly. Before getting to that, let me explain how this approach fails to answer Dan's question.

It does **NOT** explicitly identify with certainty the business keys stored in an application system.

What it does do, which was unexpected, is identify the columns that are absolutely **NOT** business keys.

I am using some made-up numbers as an example. Given an application with 100 tables, each table has ten columns. This application uses 1,000 columns. Applying this approach and being generous with a few assumptions about reference tables, one could identify 900 columns with low column entropy, leaving only 100 columns to analyze.

In a very short period, the architect has narrowed down the possibilities. To further narrow down the possibilities of business keys, look at the 12 tables, each of those 100 columns that remain is part of. If the architect has done a data structure graph analysis on the ERD, and only four of those tables whose columns have high entropy have themselves a high eigenvector centrality, the architect has narrowed down the list of 100 to no more than 40.

Instead of looking for a needle in a haystack, the architect brought a gas can to the haystack and, using a little math, burned away the detritus, leaving only interesting artifacts worthy of study.

The previous section was instrumental specifically for data vault implementations. The following is an example of using the Column Entropy Similarity algorithm to split one table into two tables.

DataType	guid	char(8)	char(8)	char(8)	int	int	int	date	date	date	varchar (4096)	varchar (4096)	varchar (4096)
Size in bytes	16	64	64	64	8	8	8	8	8	8	32,768	32,768	32,768
Total Size	98,560												
Number of rows	1,000,000												
Total Size in Bytes	98,560,000,000												
Total Size in Meg	93,994.14												
Total Size in Gig	91.79												

DataType	guid	char(8)	char(8)	int	date	date	varchar (4096)	nguid
Size in bytes	16	64	64	8	8	8	32,768	16
Total Size	32,952							
Number of rows	700,000							
Total Size in Bytes	23,066,400,000							
Total Size in Meg	21,997.83							
Total Size in Gig	21.48							

DataType	nguid	char(8)	int	int	date	varchar (4096)	varchar (4096)
Size in bytes	16	64	8	8	8	32,768	32,768
Total Size	65,640						
Number of rows	150,000						
Total Size in Bytes	9,846,000,000						
Total Size in Meg	9,389.88						
Total Size in Gig	9.17						

I am using the example from a previous section on joining together like data types in groupings. In this example, one table becomes two. Using the rate of change analysis, instead of one million records, this table is split into two tables, one of 700k and one of 150k. The space utilization goes from 91 Gig to a total of 31 Gig.

What would the performance difference be in querying one table that was 91 gigs versus two tables that were 30 gigs, even if a new column were introduced to join them?

Remember the section on volumetrics? Imagine combining this information with the tools you already have to be able to estimate the size of the data that must be available to meet your business requirements.

Dimensional Data Model

"Dimensions provide the "who, what, where, when, why, and how." context surrounding a business process event. Dimension tables contain the descriptive attributes used by BI applications for filtering and grouping the facts." - Ralph Kimball

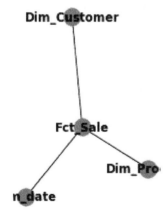

A dimensional data model is a specific type of data modeling approach used in the field of data warehousing and business intelligence (BI) to organize and represent data for efficient querying and analysis. It is designed to support online analytical processing (OLAP) and enable users to explore and analyze data for decision-making purposes quickly. The dimensional data model primarily consists of two key components: dimensions and facts.

Dimension tables are the descriptive attributes or characteristics of the data that provide context for analysis. They represent the different ways data can be sliced and diced to gain insights. Dimensions are typically hierarchical and are used for grouping and organizing data.

Fact tables are the quantitative data points or metrics that focus analysis. They represent the measurable aspects of the business, such as sales revenue, profit, quantity sold, or any other performance indicators. Facts are typically stored in a fact table and are associated with dimension keys that link them to dimension tables.

In a dimensional data model, surrogate keys join dimension tables to fact tables and establish the relationship between dimensions and facts. These relationships allow users to navigate through the data along different dimensions, making it easy to answer complex analytical questions.

The best book I have found to learn dimensional modeling is "The Data Warehouse Toolkit".[42]

Dimensional data modeling is the best data modeling technique for quickly reporting known information with many options.

---

[42] https://www.amazon.com/Data-Warehouse-Toolkit-Definitive-Dimensional/dp/1118530802

I started dimensional data modeling in late 2004. Before my introduction to this technique, every report that ran in the production database I supported had a custom-built set of tables to support a single report.

Election night 2004 was the moment when I understood how a dimensional model could support robust, detailed reporting.

In a United States Federal election, each district has its own process for counting votes. Some states or counties start counting votes as soon as a ballot arrives. This means that on election day, for those voting early or absentee, the election administrators already have a count of which candidate for which position has how many votes.

Some localities take the primitive, backward approach of only starting to count on the morning of election day when the polls open. Localities with fewer resources send their chain of custody-controlled packages of votes to localities with the resources. They collect the ballots and then send them to a central counting facility on election night. This lack of a universal standard can cause some chaos, as well as conspiracy wingnuts making claims of fraud because they do not take the time to learn and understand the process.

The state votes are rolled up and shown on network television at the federal level. When I was watching the results coming in on election night of 2004, the question I had in mind was: How are they rolling up the data so quickly?

Attempting to apply the techniques I had recently learned to the election, I began running some mental scenarios.

Suppose you have a few dimensions: DIM_Candidate, DIM_Voter, DIM_Position, DIM_Date, and DIM_Time. Add to that a single fact table FCT_VOTE. You can roll up the same data differently with some simple queries and get consistent results.

DIM_Candidate would identify all the candidates across the United States with their surrogate keys. DIM_Voter would contain the actual voters, along with their demographic information and party affiliation. DIM_Position would include the positions (Texas Senator, Kentucky State Congressperson District N, Virginia Congressperson District X). DIM_Date and DIM_Time would contain calendar and wall-clock information.

The fact table is then the only thing that is really updated for visualization purposes. New records are sent to the fact table every few minutes, hour, or other period of time. Once populated with the same query, the only difference being the where clause, you could report **all** the information across **all** districts, states, districts, or counties.

You can do all of this from **six** tables!

I have been in positions throughout my career where I reported to individuals with a heavy application development background with almost no fundamental understanding of data modeling, data architecture, or the capabilities of what we can do with a well-thought-out set of data structures.

In one such case, I had a manager who gave us some code we needed to deploy that was little more than a prototype from a business analyst. I explained the performance problems we would encounter promoting this code. I suggested we restructure the application into a dimensional model with some lightweight code on top of it.

After carefully explaining the amount of time and effort required to implement this and how wasting time on it would prevent us from making a more general solution, he clearly had yet to learn what I was talking about.

He claimed that implementing the application-based solution was more general purpose than "wasting time" creating tables. The question then became, "Well, how many reports can your data structures create? It cannot be more than this."

I did not have an answer at the time. To find one, I needed a new tool: I needed to learn how to count.

Combinatorics

Combinatorics "is, without doubt, one of the hardest in which to write an effective exposition. The reason for this is the fact that so much of the material occurs in an isolated fashion in so many different applications both to pure and applied mathematics and to other fields. Combinatorial analysis is a subject in which many of the fundamental results are frequently rediscovered by people in different fields, from first principles." - Frank Harary.

Combinatorics is the study of the ways of counting things. In some ways, the example I gave at the beginning with Gauss was an example of combinatorics. There are many ways to sum the values of 1 to 100. Gauss figured out a way to sum the values for his assignment that his teacher did not anticipate.

I need to run through a few definitions of some terms used in combinatorics before showing the application to understand more about dimensional modeling.

Combinatorics is a branch of mathematics that deals with counting and arranging objects. It is used in many fields, such as computer science, statistics, and physics. In this section, we will introduce the basic concepts of combinatorics and provide examples to help you better understand them.

The Fundamental Counting Principle

The Fundamental Counting Principle is a basic principle in combinatorics that helps us count the number of ways we can combine objects. The principle states that if there are n ways to do one thing and m ways to do another, then there are n x m ways to do both. We can extend this principle to more than two actions by multiplying the number of ways to do each action.

Example 1: Suppose you have two shirts and three pairs of pants. How many different outfits can you make?

Using the Fundamental Counting Principle, we can count the number of outfits as follows:

- There are 2 ways to choose a shirt.
- There are 3 ways to choose a pair of pants.

Therefore, the total number of outfits is 2 x 3 = 6.

Example 2: Suppose you have a four-digit combination lock. Each digit can be any number from 0 to 9. How many combinations are there?

Using the Fundamental Counting Principle, we can count the number of combinations as follows:

- There are 10 ways to choose the first digit (0-9).
- There are 10 ways to choose the second digit (0-9).
- There are 10 ways to choose the third digit (0-9).
- There are 10 ways to choose the fourth digit (0-9).

Therefore, the total number of combinations is 10 x 10 x 10 x 10 = 10,000.

Permutations

A permutation is an arrangement of a set of objects in a specific order. The number of permutations of a set of n objects is given by n!, which is the product of all positive integers up to n.

Example 3: Suppose you have four letters: A, B, C, and D. How many ways can you arrange them?

Using the formula for permutations, we can count the number of arrangements as follows:

- There are 4 choices for the first letter.
- There are 3 choices for the second letter (since we have already used one letter).
- There are 2 choices for the third letter (since we have already used two letters).
- There is only 1 choice for the fourth letter (since we have already used three letters).

Therefore, the total number of arrangements is 4 x 3 x 2 x 1 = 24.

Combinations

A combination is a selection of objects from a set without regard to order. The number of combinations of n objects taken r at a time is given by the formula C(n,r) = n! / (r! (n-r)!). I have also heard this referred to by the name of "N choose K." Another notation for this is: $\binom{n}{k}$

Example 4: Suppose you have six people, and you want to choose a committee of three people. How many different committees can be formed?

Using the formula for combinations, we can count the number of committees as follows:

C(6,3) = 6! / (3! (6-3)!) = 6 x 5 x 4 / 3 x 2 x 1 = 20

Also known as $\binom{6}{3} = 20$

Therefore, 20 different committees of three people can be formed.

Other important concepts

Another of the most fundamental concepts in combinatorics is the multiplication principle. This principle states that if there are m ways to do one thing and n ways to do another thing, then there are m x n ways to do both things.

For example, imagine that you have a choice of 3 different-colored shirts and 2 different-colored pants. Using the multiplication principle, you can see that there are 3 x 2 = 6 outfits you can create using these shirts and pants.

Another critical concept in combinatorics is permutations. Permutations refer to the number of ways that objects can be arranged in a specific order.

For example, imagine you have 3 different Lego blocks: a red block, a blue block, and a green block. You can arrange them in 6 different ways:

1. Red, blue, green
2. Red, green, blue
3. Blue, red, green
4. Blue, green, red
5. Green, red, blue
6. Green, blue, red

The formula for permutations is n!/(n-r)! where n is the total number of objects and r is the number of objects you want to arrange.

A third concept is combinations. Combinations refer to the number of ways that objects can be arranged without regard to order.

For example, imagine you have 5 different fruits: apples, bananas, oranges, pears, and strawberries. You can pick 3 of these fruits, but you need to care in what order you pick them. The number of combinations is 10:

1. Apples, bananas, oranges
2. Apples, bananas, pears
3. Apples, bananas, strawberries
4. Apples, oranges, pears
5. Apples, oranges, strawberries
6. Apples, pears, strawberries
7. Bananas, oranges, pears
8. Bananas, oranges, strawberries
9. Bananas, pears, strawberries
10. Oranges, pears, strawberries

The formula for combinations is $n!/r!(n-r)!$, where n is the total number of objects and r is the number of objects you want to choose.

Lastly, another concept in combinatorics is the principle of inclusion-exclusion. This principle is used when counting events that can happen in multiple ways. To find the total number of ways something can happen, you need to add up the number of times it can occur in each way and then subtract the cases where it can happen in both ways to avoid double counting.

For example, imagine you have 10 different toys in a toy box. Some of them are stuffed animals, and some of them are action figures. You want to count the number of toys that are either a stuffed animal or an action figure. There are 6 stuffed animals and 4 action figures, but 2 toys are both stuffed animals and action figures. Using the inclusion-exclusion principle, you can see that the total number of toys that are either a stuffed animal or an action figure is 6 + 4 - 2 = 8.

Whew! Hopefully, those explanations were straightforward enough without going too far over the top.

Now, we will apply some of these techniques to counting the number of queries that a single table can produce. Given a table with five columns, how many basic select statements can we perform against this data without transforming any of the columns using SQL functions?

Using the mechanism for counting of N choose K, we will get the following:

$$\binom{5}{0} + \binom{5}{1} + \binom{5}{2} + \binom{5}{3} + \binom{5}{4} + \binom{5}{5}$$

$$1 \quad +5 \quad +10 \quad +10 \quad +5 \quad +1 == 32$$

At least a couple of things came to mind when I first did this calculation:

- There is no way to select *no columns* from a table.

- I have seen a relationship between 5 and 32 before.

- Each of these sequential numbers produced by summarizing the number of N choose K values for any given N is an aspect of the binomial theorem called the binomial coefficient, whose understanding I will leave as an exercise to the interested reader[43].

The relationship between 5 and 32 is: $2^5 = 32$ and since a select statement must have at least 1 column in the select clause, we will have to remove the result of $\binom{5}{0}$ which produces:

$$2^5 - 1 = 31$$

We derive this expression by working with the binomial theorem, and can generalize it to any table.

$$2^C - 1$$

The answer to the question of "How many select statements can be produced from a single table using only the base columns defined for the table with no transformation?" is therefore:

$$2^C - 1$$

In other words, 2 raised to the power of the number of columns minus one.

But this is only for a single table. How many queries can a dimensional model produce? I needed to add some qualifiers to this expression to leverage it properly:

- Key columns, either Primary or foreign keys, should not be part of the select.

---

[43] https://en.wikipedia.org/wiki/Binomial_theorem

- Metadata columns should not be part of the selection.

- Fact table measures must also be considered.

Building on some of the graph work I had done previously, I realized that for each table, I had to multiply the result of this expression by the result of the expression to which it is connected. We then multiply this entire result by the number of measures in the fact tables to which they are associated.

Now, drum roll please, to calculate the number of select queries that a dimensional model can produce, the expression is:

$$M \prod_i^n (2^{c_i} - 1)$$

M is the number of measures.

i is the number of the table, and c_i is the number of columns for the table number i.

Now that we have done a decent amount of math, is there any other conclusion we can draw from this analysis?

This analysis supports the claim that a dimensional data model is a combinatorial object. Putting on our abstract glasses, we now have identified how many queries to do from a structural perspective. If we look at the values represented in the descriptive columns of the dimensions, using a dimensional model allows for the combinatorial analysis of measures identified in the fact table(s).

This is such a fundamental component of the dimensional model that explains why, for decades, tool vendors working in the business intelligence space have both requested and demanded a dimensional model.

The phenomenal works done by Bill Inmon and Ralph Kimball, in which each of them explains the mechanics of dimensional modeling, all come down to "How to do dimensional modeling."

My claim is: The above explains, "This is why dimensional modeling works so well."

To be consistent with what was done previously for data vault structures, a dimensional model represented in mathematical notation becomes:

$$P_d(x_1, \ldots, x_n) \rightarrow f(x) \leftarrow P_c(x_1, \ldots x_n)$$

After a short diversion into economics and the performance of various components of a data ecosystem, we will revisit database design using some of the tools we have developed throughout this work.

Economics

"Among the social sciences, economists are the snobs. Economics, with its numbers, graphs, and curves, at least has the coloration and paraphernalia of a hard science. It's not just putting on sandals and trekking out to take notes on some tribe." - Michael Kinsley

Economics is the study of how people make choices in the face of scarcity or constraints. Scarcity occurs when people want more goods and services than are available. In this situation, people must choose which needs to be fulfilled and which to leave out. They make decisions based on their self-interest, weighing costs and benefits.

Scarcity and choices

At the core of economics lies the concept of scarcity. Scarcity refers to the fundamental problem that arises because our wants and needs are limitless, while the resources available to fulfill these desires are limited. This scarcity necessitates choices and trade-offs. Individuals, firms, and societies must decide how to allocate their limited resources efficiently to maximize utility and achieve their objectives.

Supply and demand curves are fundamental concepts in economics that help explain how to determine prices and quantities of goods and services in a market. These curves illustrate the relationship between a product's price and the amount producers are willing to supply and consumers are eager to buy. Let us break down the mathematics of supply and demand curves and how they interact with each other.

The demand curve

The demand curve represents the relationship between the price of a good and the quantity that reasonable consumers are willing to purchase at various prices, assuming other factors remain constant. Mathematically, the demand curve can be represented as:

$$Q_d = f(P)$$

Where:

- Q_d is the quantity demanded.
- P is the price of the good.
- $f(P)$ is a function that describes how the quantity demanded changes with price.

The demand curve is typically downward-sloping, meaning that as the price P increases, the quantity demanded decreases, and vice versa. This relationship is often explained by the law of demand, which states that all else being equal, as the price of a good rises, the quantity demanded decreases, and as the price falls, the quantity demanded increases.

The supply curve

The supply curve represents the relationship between the price of a good and the quantity of that good producers are willing to supply at various prices, assuming other factors remain constant. Mathematically, the supply curve can be represented as:

$$Q_s = g(P)$$

Where:

- Q_s is the quantity supplied.
- P is the price of the good.
- $g(P)$ is a function that describes how the quantity supplied changes with price.

The supply curve is typically upward-sloping, meaning that as the price P increases, the quantity supplied Q_s also increases, and vice versa. This relationship is often explained by the law of supply, which states that, all else being equal, as the price of a good rises, the quantity supplied increases, and as the price falls, the quantity supplied decreases.

Equilibrium

The point where the demand and supply curves intersect is called the equilibrium point. At this point, the quantity demanded Q_d equals the quantity supplied Q_s, and the market is in equilibrium. Mathematically, this equilibrium condition can be expressed as:

$$Q_d = Q_s$$

At this equilibrium price P^* and quantity Q^*, the market clears, meaning that all buyers who want to buy at that price can do so, and all sellers who wish to sell at that price can do so.

Shifts in supply and demand

In the real world, supply and demand are influenced by various factors, such as changes in consumer preferences, technology, government policies, and more. When any of these factors change, the demand or supply curve can shift.

- **Shift in demand:** If something causes an increase in demand, the demand curve shifts to the right. This means that at any given price, consumers are willing to buy more of the product, leading to a higher equilibrium price and quantity. Conversely, a decrease in demand shifts the demand curve to the left.

- **Shift in supply**: If something causes an increase in supply, the supply curve shifts to the right. This means that at any given price, producers are willing to supply more of the product, leading to a lower equilibrium price and a higher quantity traded. Conversely, a decrease in supply shifts the supply curve to the left.

These shifts in supply and demand can cause changes in equilibrium price and quantity.

One of the most well-known economics image is the demand-supply curve.

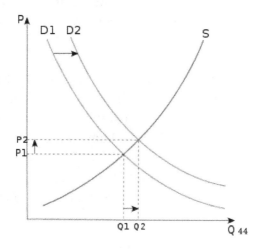

---

[44] https://en.wikipedia.org/wiki/Supply_and_demand

This is considered an idealized graph. As in everything when going from mathematics to the "real world," there are nuances in price, availability, demand, need, utility, and other things that are not always easy to capture. These nuances keep economists employed as they work to explain the phenomena of human behavior in consumer markets.

The following image is one I created a few years ago for a blog post about performance relationships between databases, networks, and reporting servers. I was in a position where I had to monitor performance across a data ecosystem periodically. When working in isolation and testing each component, I could see how each component's performance footprint changed.

It was different from sitting in the computer room as a teenager and hearing the mechanical noises of the mainframe components using more resources than if they were sitting idle. I was watching the output of performance utilities on a database server and a business intelligence server.

Each of these components was running in "isolation," but they were communicating with each other. When one did something, the others responded in kind according to their abilities. In a tiny act of hubris, I am going to quote myself from a blog I wrote before. I will elaborate on this, considering some new things I have learned. This chart needs a little context to understand the relationships between the four quadrants.

Quadrant I is the server network bandwidth. In a typical linear relationship, as the data size increases from the database to the front end, the server network bandwidth increases.

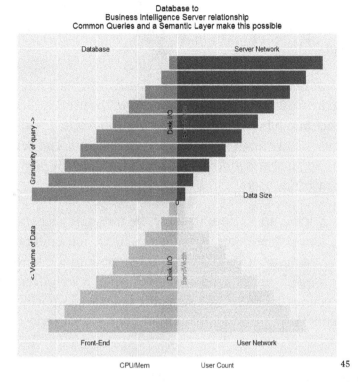

Quadrant II is the database performance relationship between CPU/Memory and Disk I/O for a varying query workload. For highly aggregated queries, the CPU and memory usage increases, and the server network bandwidth is smaller because less data is being put on the wire. For less aggregated data and more full data transfers, the Disk I/O is higher, memory is lower, and back in Quadrant I, the Server Network Bandwidth is higher.

---

[45] https://the-data-guy.blogspot.com/2017/01/what-is-performance-relationship.html

Quadrant III is the front-end server performance comparing CPU/Memory and Disk I/O when dealing with a varying volume of data. As the data from the database increases, more resources and caching are needed on this server.

Quadrant IV is the User Network Bandwidth, which results from the front-end server responding to the user's requests. As the number of users increases, the volume of data increases and more of a load is put on the front-end server. Likewise, the bandwidth increases as more data is provided to the various users.

This image is an attempt to show the interactions between these four components. Architects who do not understand the interaction between these four components build shitty systems. This image is possible because of a well-designed dimensional model, a rich semantic layer with appropriate business definitions, and common queries that tend to be repeated.

This architecture can support exploratory analysis. However, we must define and load up front the data to be explored. Exploratory analysis should determine which data points to include in the data mart, which we should do in a separate environment.

I created all three of these images with R using iGraph and ggplot2 with anecdotal data. The data shown in this chart is not sampled but is meant to represent how these four systems interact. Having experience monitoring many platforms supporting this architecture, I know that no production systems will show these rises and falls the way this representative chart is doing.

Database Design Revisited

Now that we have synthesized some advanced mathematics with our data structures, here are some guidelines for using these techniques to enrich the data structure design process.

- Application databases MUST be physically separate from databases that support integration, reporting, and analysis.

- Once a database has been designed and is collecting information, use the column entropy measure to validate that all the columns in the tables have a similar rate of change. This will significantly impact storage utilization.

- In a few of my presentations, I jokingly refer to the following as "Doug's performance law." What does not get organized with a data structure must get organized with application code, and data structures are more efficient!

- The best-performing bit of code is the code that is never run.

- Use graph tools to analyze the database's design. Which tables have higher centrality? Is that what is expected?

- If you are writing a reporting application and using anything other than a dimensional model to make the reporting more general-purpose, you are simply wrong!

- The volume of data will continue to grow. Soon, universal laws such as the speed of light will negatively impact the ability to move and transform data. As the volume increases, we must prepare the data so that it can be used for more than one purpose. These mathematical tools will help us determine the best structures to support many use cases.

- The data in the database represents something. It represents human behavior.

Anthropology

"What one generation tolerates, the next generation will embrace." - John Wesley

Why do we capture data at all?

People.

Whether we admit it or not, our businesses make money by studying the behavior of other humans. How, when, where, what, and who is buying something? We can argue that analyzing things like supply chains or product costs does not relate to the behavior of other humans. I will make another mention of the law of comparative advantage.[46] This is the heart of why we have things like supply chains. One group of people or country is better at making a thing than another country or group of people. Sometimes raw resources for making a thing are only in one physical

---

[46] https://en.wikipedia.org/wiki/Comparative_advantage

location. That raw resource needs to be shipped to another location and transformed from a raw material into a new product. Thus supply chains exist because the consumer drives the demand for a product and some other group of humans knows that this desire exists, so they become the *supplier*.

However, anthropology is a social science that studies humans and their societies, cultures, and behaviors. It encompasses a wide range of disciplines, including socio-cultural anthropology, archaeology, linguistic anthropology, and biological anthropology. While anthropology has traditionally been associated with academic research and ethnographic fieldwork, its principles and methodologies have found significant applicability in various fields, including business.

Anthropology is a broad field that encompasses various subfields, including cultural anthropology, biological anthropology, archaeology, and linguistic anthropology.

Biological anthropology, also known as physical anthropology, focuses on the biological and evolutionary aspects of human beings. It explores human origins, human variation, and the relationship between biology and culture. Biological anthropologists may study human fossils, genetics, primatology, and human adaptations to different environments.

Archaeology involves studying human history and prehistory through the excavation and analysis of artifacts, structures, and other physical remains. Archaeologists uncover and interpret evidence to reconstruct past societies, technological advancements, and cultural practices.

Linguistic anthropology examines the role of language in human societies. It explores the structure, variation, and evolution of language and how language influences and shapes human thought, social interactions, and cultural practices.

Cultural anthropology examines the beliefs, behaviors, and social structures of different societies and cultures. It focuses on understanding how people create meaning, communicate, and organize themselves within their cultural contexts. This can involve studying rituals, kinship systems, economic practices, political structures, and more.

Culture evolves. To highlight its changing nature, let me list a few things that have changed since I was younger.

Minnesota adopted the first smoking restriction in 1975 under the Minnesota Clean Indoor Air Act, which restricted smoking in most public places. Many states followed, initially making separate smoking sections indoors, which then shifted to altogether banning all smoking from indoor and public areas. Smoking was banned from all airline flights beginning and ending in the U.S. in November of 1989.

Before 2007, there were no state laws regarding distracted driving in relation to texting on a cell phone. In 2007, Washington became the first state to pass a texting ban. As of 2014, text messaging for all drivers has been banned in 41 states.

While laws vary from state to state, driving a car without wearing a seat belt was once legal. New York was the first state to pass a law requiring vehicle occupants to wear seat belts in 1984. Today, there are mandatory seat belt laws for adults in all states except New Hampshire.

Laws should reflect a society's evolving culture. This is only sometimes the case. Some want to make laws to force things to be the way they individually think they need to be. Culture has moved on. Separate drinking fountains would no longer be tolerated today, even if they were "legal." Those of us involved in the purchasing patterns, the interacting patterns, and the general behavior of society can watch the evolution of our culture.

While this has been a very technical book, and it needs to be, we should remember that the growth of data and the changes in our cultures will continue to evolve. We must build our data ecosystems to anticipate and react to cultural changes.

Having a well-designed data ecosystem will allow us to do that. Also, business scientists, data scientists, and people who study the data collected by our enterprises should be aware of the limitations of looking at data with a cultural bias. Predicting how our organizations should do things based on a limited understanding of the cultural diversity of our customers, clients, and prospects will produce outcomes that will only make sense once we include these concepts in our overall approach.

Anthropology's scope is broad, encompassing research on every continent and across diverse cultural, historical, and social contexts. Anthropologists conduct fieldwork, engage in ethnographic observations, interview individuals, gather data, and analyze information to better understand the diversity of human societies and the similarities that bind us as a species. The discipline also seeks to explore the connections between different aspects of human life, such as culture, biology, language, and history, to gain a more comprehensive understanding of the human experience.

It is important to note that these sub-disciplines often overlap with each other, and many anthropologists may engage in interdisciplinary research that draws from multiple sub-disciplines. Additionally, there are niche or specialized areas within each sub-discipline, reflecting the wide range of topics and interests within the field of anthropology.

With the plethora of available data, businesses must comprehend the underlying reasons behind product purchases. A thorough analysis of customer purchase behavior is crucial to gain this understanding. It is essential to recognize that our customers are fellow humans, influenced by their culture, society, and behavior. These factors significantly impact their purchasing habits and ultimately affect our company's bottom line. Until we cater to extraterrestrial visitors, we must acknowledge the human element in our customer base and its profound impact on our business success.

This is what our data structures represent: the synthesis between human behavior, data structure implementation, and advanced mathematics.

Humans are diverse. Everyone faces their own challenges. Organizing our growing data collections in such a manner to be able to understand these diverse challenges will only make us all stronger.

Above all, our data represents humans.

Index

www.ingramcontent.com/pod-product-compliance
Lightning Source LLC
Chambersburg PA
CBHW071237050326
40690CB00011B/2157